acute and less severe, indeed, than the present race. As a testimony—they often had not satire sharp enough to avert that bitterest punishment to an ambitious author—neglect.

Of this play, "Every One has his Fault," nothing, in modesty, can be said, beyond mere matter of fact. It has been productive both to the manager and the writer, having, on its first appearance, run, in the theatrical term, near thirty nights; during which, some of the audience were heard to laugh, and some were seen to weep—it may likewise with truth be added, that, whatever critics may please to say against the production, they cannot think more humbly of its worth, than

THE AUTHOR.

DRAMATIS PERSONÆ

Lord Norland	Mr. Farren.
Sir Robert Ramble	Mr. Lewis.
Mr. Solus	Mr. Quick.
Mr. Harmony	Mr. Munden.
Mr. Placid	Mr. Fawcett.
Mr. Irwin	Mr. Pope.
Hammond	Mr. Powell.
Porter	Mr. Thompson.
Edward	Miss Grist.

Lady Eleanor Irwin	Mrs. Pope.
Mrs. Placid	Mrs. Mattocks.
Miss Spinster	Mrs. Webb.
Miss Wooburn	Mrs. Esten.

Servants, &c.

SCENE:—London.

EVERY ONE HAS HIS FAULT

ACT THE FIRST

SCENE I

An Apartment at Mr. Placid's

Enter **MR PLACID** and **MR SOLUS**.

MR PLACID

You are to blame.

MR SOLUS
I say the same by you.

MR PLACID
And yet your singularity pleases me; for you are the first elderly bachelor I ever knew, who did not hug himself in the reflection, that he was not in the trammels of wedlock.

MR SOLUS
No; I am only the first elderly bachelor who has truth and courage enough, to confess his dissatisfaction.

MR PLACID
And you really wish you were married?

MR SOLUS
I do. I wish still more, that I had been married thirty years ago. Oh! I wish that a wife and half a score children would now start up around me, and bring along with them all that affection, which we should have had for each other by being earlier acquainted. But as it is, in my present state, there is not a person in the world I care a straw for;—and the world is pretty even with me, for I don't believe there is a creature in it who cares a straw for me.

MR PLACID
Pshaw! You have in your time been a man of gallantry; and, consequently, must have made many attachments.

MR SOLUS
Yes, such as men of gallantry usually make. I have been attached to women, who have purloined my fortune, and to men, who have partaken of the theft: I have been in as much fear of my mistress, as you are of your wife.

MR PLACID
Is that possible?

MR SOLUS
Yes; and without having one of those tender, delicate, ties of a husband, an excuse for my apprehension.—I have maintained children—

MR PLACID
Then why do you complain for the want of a family?

MR SOLUS
I did not say, I ever had any children; I said, I had maintained them; but I never believed they were mine; for I could have no dependence upon the principles of their mother—and never did I take one of those tender infants in my arms, that the forehead of my valet, the squint eye of my apothecary, or the double chin of my chaplain, did not stare me in the face, and damp all the fine feelings of the parent, which I had just called up.

Every One Has His Fault by Mrs Inchbald

A COMEDY, IN FIVE ACTS

AS PERFORMED AT THE THEATRE ROYAL, COVENT GARDEN

Elizabeth Simpson was born on 15th October 1753 at Stanningfield, near Bury St Edmunds, Suffolk.

Despite the fact that she suffered from a debilitating stammer she was determined to become an actress.

In April 1772, Elizabeth left, without permission, for London to pursue her chosen career. Although she was successful in obtaining parts her audiences, at first, found it difficult to admire her talents given her speech impediment. However, Elizabeth was diligent and hard-working on attempting to overcome this hurdle. She spent much time concentrating on pronunciation in order to eliminate the stammer. Her acting, although at times stilted, especially in monologues, gained praise for her approach for her well-developed characters.

That same year she married Joseph Inchbald and a few months later they appeared for the first time together on stage in 'King Lear'. The following month they toured Scotland with the West Digges's theatre company. This was to continue for several years.

Completely unexpectedly Joseph died in June 1779. It was now in the years after her husband's death that Elizabeth decided on a new literary path. With no attachments and acting taking up only some of her time she decided to write plays.

Her first play to be performed was 'A Mogul Tale or, The Descent of the Balloon', in 1784, in which she also played the leading female role of Selina. The play was premiered at the Haymarket Theatre.

One of the things that separated Elizabeth from other contemporary playwrights was her ability to translate plays from German and French into English for an audience that was ever-hungry for new works.

Her success as a playwright enabled Elizabeth to support herself and have no need of a husband to support her. Between 1784 and 1805 she had 19 of her comedies, sentimental dramas, and farces (many of them translations from the French) performed at London theatres. She is usually credited as Mrs Inchbald.

Mrs Elizabeth Inchbald died on 1st August 1821 in Kensington, London.

Index of Contents

REMARKS

There is at present an opinion prevailing, in regard to dramatic works, which, if just, is wholly contradictory to every proof of cause and effect, which has been applied to the rise and fall of other arts, and sciences.

It is said, that modern dramas are the worst that ever appeared on the English stage—yet it is well known, that the English theatres never flourished as they do at present.

When it is inquired, why painting, poetry, and sculpture, decline in England? "Want of encouragement," is the sure reply—but this reply cannot be given to the question, "Why dramatic literature fails?" for never was there such high remuneration conferred upon every person, and every work, belonging to the drama.

A new play, which, from a reputed wit of former times, would not, with success, bring him a hundred pounds, a manager will now purchase, from a reputed blockhead, at the price of near a thousand; and sustain all risk whether it be condemned or not.

Great must be the attraction of modern plays, to repay such speculation.

It follows, then, if the stage be really sunk so low as it is said to be, that patronage and reward have ruined, instead of having advanced, genius. Or, is it not more likely, that public favour has incited the envious to rail; or, at best, raised up minute inquirers into the excellence of that amusement, which charms a whole nation; and criticism sees faults, as fear sees ghosts—whenever they are looked for.

It is a consolation to the dramatist of the present age, that, while his plays are more attractive than ever those of former writers were, those authors had their contemporary critics as well as he; though less

MR PLACID

But those are accidents, which may occur in the marriage state.

MR SOLUS

In that case, a man is pitied—in mine, he is only laughed at.

MR PLACID

I wish to heaven I could exchange the pity which my friends bestow on me, for the merriment which your ill fate excites.

MR SOLUS

You want but courage to be envied.

MR PLACID

Does any one doubt my courage?

MR SOLUS

No; if a prince were to offend you, you would challenge him—

MR PLACID

But if my wife offend me, I am obliged to make an apology.—Was not that her voice? I hope she has not overheard our conversation.

MR SOLUS

If she have, she'll be in an ill humour.

MR PLACID

That she will be, whether she have heard it or not.

MR SOLUS

Well, good day. I don't like to be driven from my fixed plan of wedlock; and, therefore, I won't be a spectator of your mutual discontent.

[Going.

MR PLACID

But before you go, Mr. Solus, permit me to remind you of a certain concern, that, I think, would afford you much more delight, than all you can, at this time of life, propose to yourself in marriage. Make happy, by your beneficence, a near relation, whom the truest affection has drawn into that state, but who is denied the blessing of competency, to make the state supportable.

MR SOLUS

You mean my nephew, Irwin? But do not you acknowledge he has a wife and children? Did not he marry the woman he loved, and has he not, at this moment, a large family, by whom he is beloved? And is he not, therefore, with all his poverty, much happier than I am? He has often told me, when I have reproached him with his indiscreet marriage, "that in his wife he possessed kingdoms!" Do you suppose I will give any part of my fortune to a man who enjoys such extensive domains? No:—let him preserve his territories, and I will keep my little estate for my own use.

[Exit.

MR PLACID
John! John!

[Enter **SERVANT**.

Has your mistress been inquiring for me?

JOHN
Yes, sir:—My lady asked, just now, if I knew who was with you?

MR PLACID
Did she seem angry?

JOHN
No, sir;—pretty well.

MR PLACID [In Anger]
You scoundrel, what do you mean by "pretty well?"

JOHN
Much as usual, sir.

MR PLACID
And do you call that "pretty well?" You scoundrel, I have a great mind—

[Enter **MRS PLACID**, speaking very loud.

MRS PLACID
What is the matter, Mr. Placid? What is all this noise about? You know I hate a noise. What is the matter?

MR PLACID
My dear, I was only finding fault with that blockhead.

MRS PLACID
Pray, Mr. Placid, do not find fault with any body in this house. But I have something which I must take you very severely to task about, sir.

MR PLACID
No, my dear, not just now, pray.

MRS PLACID
Why not now?

MR PLACID [Looking at his Watch]

Because dinner will be ready in a very few minutes. I am very hungry, and it will be cruel of you to spoil my appetite. John, is the dinner on table?

MRS PLACID

No, John, don't let it be served yet—Mr. Placid, you shall first hear what I have to say.

[Sitting down.—Exit **SERVANT**.

MR PLACID

But then I know I shall not be able to eat a morsel.

MRS PLACID

Sit down.

[**MR PLACID** sits.

—I believe, Mr. Placid, you are going to do a very silly thing. I am afraid you are going to lend some money?

MR PLACID

Well, my dear, and suppose I am?

MRS PLACID

Then, I don't approve of people lending their money.

MR PLACID

But, my dear, I have known you approve of borrowing money: and, once in our lives, what should we have done, if every body had refused to lend.

MRS PLACID

That is nothing to the purpose.—And, now, I desire you will hear what I say, without speaking a word yourself.

MR PLACID

Well, my dear.

MRS PLACID

Now, mind you don't speak, till I have done.—Our old acquaintance, Captain Irwin, and Lady Eleanor, his wife (with whom we lived upon very intimate terms, to be sure, while we were in America), are returned to London; and, I find, you have visited them very frequently.

MR PLACID

Not above two or three times, upon my word; for it hurts me to see them in distress, and I forbear to go.

MRS PLACID

There! you own they are in distress; I expected as much. Now, own to me that they have asked you to lend them money.

MR PLACID
I do own it—I do own it. Now, are you satisfied?

MRS PLACID
No: for I have no doubt but you have promised they shall have it.

MR PLACID
No, upon my word I have not promised.

MRS PLACID
Then promise me they shall not.

MR PLACID
Nay, my dear, you have no idea of their unhappy situation.

MRS PLACID
Yes, I have; and 'tis that which makes me suspicious.

MR PLACID
His regiment is now broken; all her jewels, and little bawbles, are disposed of; and he is in such dread of his old creditors, that, in the lodging they have taken, he passes by the name of Middleton—They have three more children, my dear, than when we left them in New York; and they have, in vain, sent repeated supplications, both to his uncle, and her father, for the smallest bounty.

MRS PLACID
And is not her father, my Lord Norland, a remarkable wise man, and a good man? and ought you to do for them, what he has refused?

MR PLACID
They have offended him, but they have never offended me.

MRS PLACID
I think, 'tis an offence, to ask a friend for money, when there is no certainty of returning it.

MR PLACID
By no means: for, if there were a certainty, even an enemy might lend.

MRS PLACID
But I insist, Mr. Placid, that they shall not find a friend in you upon this occasion.—What do you say, sir?

MR PLACID [After a Struggle]
No, my dear, they shall not.

MRS PLACID
Positively shall not?

MR PLACID
Positively shall not—since they have found an enemy in you.

[Enter **SERVANT**.

SERVANT
Dinner is on table.

MR PLACID
Ah! I am not hungry now.

MRS PLACID
What do you mean by that, Mr. Placid? I insist on your being hungry.

MR PLACID
Oh, yes! I have a very excellent appetite. I shall eat prodigiously.

MRS PLACID
You had better.

[Exeunt.

An Apartment at Mr. Harmony's

Enter **MR HARMONY**, followed by **MISS SPINSTER**.

MISS SPINSTER
Cousin, cousin Harmony, I will not forgive you, for thus continually speaking in the behalf of every servant whom you find me offended with. Your philanthropy becomes insupportable; and, instead of being a virtue, degenerates into a vice.

MR HARMONY
Dear madam, do not upbraid me for a constitutional fault.

MISS SPINSTER
Very true; you had it from your infancy. I have heard your mother say, you were always foolishly tender hearted, and never showed one of those discriminating passions of envy, hatred, or revenge, to which all her other children were liable.

MR HARMONY
No: since I can remember, I have felt the most unbounded affection for all my fellow creatures. I even protest to you, dear madam, that, as I walk along the streets of this large metropolis, so warm is my heart towards every person who passes me, that I long to say, "How do you do?" and, "I am glad to see you," to them all. Some men, I should like even to stop, and shake hands with;—and some women, I should like even to stop, and kiss.

MISS SPINSTER
How can you be so ridiculous!

MR HARMONY
Nay, 'tis truth: and I sincerely lament, that human beings should be such strangers to one another as we are! We live in the same street, without knowing one another's necessities; and oftentimes meet and part from each other at church, at coffeehouses, playhouses, and all public places,—without ever speaking a single word, or nodding "Good b'ye!" though 'tis a hundred chances to ten we never see one another again.

MISS SPINSTER
Let me tell you, kinsman, all this pretended philanthropy renders you ridiculous. There is not a fraud, a theft, or hardly any vice committed, that you do not take the criminal's part, shake your head, and cry, "Provisions are so scarce!" And no longer ago than last Lord Mayor's Day, when you were told that Mr. Alderman Ravenous was ill with an indigestion, you endeavoured to soften the matter, by exclaiming, "Provisions are so scarce!"—But, above all, I condemn that false humanity, which induces you to say many things in conversation, which deserve to stigmatize you with the character of deceit.

MR HARMONY
This is a weakness, I confess. But though my honour sometimes reproaches me with it, my conscience never does: for it is by this very failing that I have frequently made the bitterest enemies friends—Just by saying a few harmless sentences, which, though a species of falsehood and deceit, yet, being soothing and acceptable to the person offended, I have immediately inspired him with lenity and forgiveness; and then, by only repeating the selfsame sentences to his opponent, I have known hearts cold and closed to each other, warmed and expanded, as every human creature's ought to be.

[Enter a **SERVANT**.

SERVANT
Mr. Solus.

[Exit **SERVANT**.

MISS SPINSTER
I cannot think, Mr. Harmony, why you keep company with that old bachelor; he is a man, of all others on earth, I dislike; and so I am obliged to quit the room, though I have a thousand things more to say.

[Exit angrily.

[Enter **MR SOLUS**.

MR HARMONY
Mr. Solus, how do you do?

MR SOLUS
I am very lonely at home; will you come and dine with me?

MR HARMONY

Now you are here, you had better stay with me: we have no company; only my cousin Miss Spinster and myself.

MR SOLUS

No, I must go home: do come to my house.

MR HARMONY

Nay, pray stay: what objection can you have?

MR SOLUS

Why, to tell you the truth, your relation, Miss Spinster, is no great favourite of mine; and I don't like to dine with you, because I don't like her company.

MR HARMONY

That is, to me, surprising!

MR SOLUS

Why, old bachelors and old maids never agree: we are too much alike in our habits: we know our own hearts so well, we are apt to discover every foible we would wish to forget, in the symptoms displayed by the other. Miss Spinster is peevish, fretful, and tiresome, and I am always in a fidget when I am in her company.

MR HARMONY

How different are her sentiments of you! for one of her greatest joys is to be in your company.

[**MR SOLUS** starts and smiles.

Poor woman! she has, to be sure, an uneven temper—

MR SOLUS

No, perhaps I am mistaken.

MR HARMONY

But I will assure you, I never see her in half such good humour as when you are here: for I believe you are the greatest favourite she has.

MR SOLUS

I am very much obliged to her, and I certainly am mistaken about her temper—Some people, if they look ever so cross, are goodnatured in the main; and I dare say she is so. Besides, she never has had a husband to sooth and soften her disposition; and there should be some allowance made for that.

MR HARMONY

Will you dine with us?

MR SOLUS

I don't care if I do. Yes, I think I will. I must however step home first:—but I'll be back in a quarter of an hour.—My compliments to Miss Spinster, if you should see her before I return.

[Exit.

[Enter **SERVANT**.

SERVANT
My lady begs to know, sir, if you have invited Mr. Solus to dine? because if you have, she shall go out.

[Exit **SERVANT**.

[Enter **MISS SPINSTER**.

MR HARMONY
Yes, madam, I could not help inviting him; for, poor man, his own house is in such a state for want of proper management, he cannot give a comfortable dinner himself.

MISS SPINSTER
And so he must spoil the comfort of mine.

MR HARMONY
Poor man! poor man! after all the praise he has been lavishing upon you!

MISS SPINSTER
What praises?

MR HARMONY
I won't tell you: for you won't believe them.

MISS SPINSTER
Yes, I shall.—Oh no—now I recollect, this is some of your invention.

MR HARMONY
Nay, I told him it was his invention; for he declared you looked better last night, than any other lady at the Opera.

MISS SPINSTER
Well, this sounds like truth:—and, depend upon it, though I never liked the manners of Mr. Solus much, yet—

MR HARMONY
Nay, Solus has his faults.

MISS SPINSTER
So we have all.

MR HARMONY
And will you leave him and me to dine by ourselves?

MISS SPINSTER

Oh no, I cannot be guilty of such ill manners, though I talked of it. Besides, poor Mr. Solus does not come so often, and it would be wrong not to show him all the civility we can. For my part, I have no dislike to the man; and, if taking a bit of dinner with us now and then can oblige either you or him, I should be to blame to make any objection. Come, let us go into the drawing-room to receive him.

MR HARMONY
Ay! this is right: this is as it should be.

[Exeunt.

SCENE III

A Room at the Lodgings of Mr. Irwin

MR IRWIN and **LADY ELEANOR IRWIN** discovered.

LADY ELEANOR
My dear husband, my dear Irwin, I cannot bear to see you thus melancholy. Is this the joy of returning to our native country, after a nine years' banishment?

MR IRWIN
Yes: For I could bear my misfortunes, my wretched poverty, with patience, in a land where our sorrows were shared by those about us; but here, in London, where plenty and ease smile upon every face; where, by your birth you claim distinction, and I by services;—here to be in want,—to be obliged to take another name, through shame of our own,—to tremble at the voice of every stranger, for fear he should be a creditor,—to meet each old acquaintance with an averted eye, because we would not feel the pang of being shunned. To have no reward for all this, even in a comfortable home; but in this our habitation, to see our children looking up to me for that support I have not in my power to give—Can I,—can I love them and you, and not be miserable?

LADY ELEANOR
Yet I am not so. And I am sure you will not doubt my love to you or them.

MR IRWIN
I met my uncle this morning, and was mean enough to repeat my request to him:—he burst into a fit of laughter, and told me my distresses were the result of my ambition, in marrying the daughter of a nobleman, who himself was too ambitious ever to pardon us.

LADY ELEANOR
Tell me no more of what he said.

MR IRWIN
This was a day of trials;—I saw your father too.

LADY ELEANOR
My father! Lord Norland! Oh Heavens!

MR IRWIN
He passed me in his carriage.

LADY ELEANOR
I envy you the blessing of seeing him! For, oh!—Excuse my tears—he is my father still.—How did he look?

MR IRWIN
As well as he did at the time I used to watch him from his house, to steal to you.—But I am sorry to acquaint you, that, to guard himself against all returning love for you, he has, I am informed, adopted a young lad, on whom he bestows every mark of that paternal affection, of which you lament the loss.

LADY ELEANOR
May the young man deserve his tenderness better than I have done—May he never disobey him—May he be a comfort, and cherish his benefactor's declining years—And when his youthful passions teach him to love, may they not, like mine, teach him disobedience!

[Enter a **SERVANT**, with a Letter.

What is that letter?

SERVANT
It comes from Mr. Placid, the servant, who brought it, said, and requires no answer.

[Exit.

MR IRWIN
It's strange how I tremble at every letter I see, as if I dreaded the contents. How poverty has unmanned me!
[Aside]
I must tell you, my dear, that finding myself left this morning without a guinea, I wrote to Mr. Placid, to borrow a small sum: This is his answer:
[Reading the Superscription]
To Mr. Middleton.—That's right: he remembers the caution I gave him. I had forgot whether I had done so, for my memory is not so good as it was. I did not even now recollect this hand, though it is one I am so well acquainted with, and ought to give me joy rather than sorrow.

[Opens the Letter hastily, reads, and lets it drop.

Now I have not a friend on earth.

LADY ELEANOR
Yes, you have me. You forget me.

MR IRWIN [In a Transport of Grief]
I would forget you—you—and all your children.

LADY ELEANOR
I would not lose the remembrance of you or of them, for all my father's fortune.

MR IRWIN
What am I to do? I must leave you! I must go, I know not whither! I cannot stay to see you perish.

[Takes his Hat, and is going.

LADY ELEANOR [Holding him]
Where would you go? 'tis evening—'tis dark—Whither would you go at this time?

MR IRWIN [Distractedly]
I must consider what's to be done—and in this room my thoughts seem too confined to reflect.

LADY ELEANOR
And are London streets calculated for reflection?

MR IRWIN
No; for action. To hurry the faint thought to resolution.

LADY ELEANOR
You are not well—Your health has been lately impaired.—Your temper has undergone a change too;—I tremble lest any accident—

MR IRWIN [Wildly]
What accident?

LADY ELEANOR
I know your provocations from an ungrateful world: But despise it: as that despises you.

MR IRWIN
But for your sake, I could.

LADY ELEANOR
Then witness, Heaven, I am happy!—Though bred in all the delicacy, the luxury of wealth and splendour; yet I have never murmured at the change of fortune, while that change has made me wife to you, and mother of your children.

MR IRWIN
We will be happy—if possible. But give me this evening to consider what plan to fix upon.—There is no time to lose: we are without friends—without money,—without credit.—Farewell for an hour.—I will see Mr. Placid, if I can; and though he have not the money to lend, he may perhaps, give me some advice.

LADY ELEANOR
Suppose I call on her?—Women are sometimes more considerate than men, and—

MR IRWIN

Do you for the best, and so will I.—Heavens bless you!

[Exeunt separately.

SCENE I

A Coffee or Club Room at a Tavern

Enter **SIR ROBERT RAMBLE—MR SOLUS** and **MR PLACID** at the opposite Side.

MR SOLUS
Sir Robert Ramble, how do you do?

SIR ROBERT
My dear Mr. Solus, I am glad to see you. I have been dining by myself, and now come into this public room, to meet with some good company.

MR SOLUS
Ay, Sir Robert, you are now reduced to the same necessity which I frequently am—I frequently am obliged to dine at taverns and coffeehouses, for want of company at home.

SIR ROBERT
I protest I am never happier than in a house like this, where a man may meet his friend without the inconvenience of form, either as a host or a visitor.

MR SOLUS
Sir Robert, give me leave to introduce to you Mr. Placid, he has been many years abroad; but I believe he now means to remain in his own country for the rest of his life. This, Mr. Placid, is Sir Robert Ramble.

SIR ROBERT [To **MR PLACID**]
Sir, I shall be happy in your acquaintance, and I assure you, if you will do me the honour to meet me now and then at this house, you will find every thing very pleasant. I verily believe that since I lost my wife, which is now about five months ago, I verily believe I have dined here three days out of the seven.

MR PLACID
Have you lost your wife, sir? And so lately?

SIR ROBERT [With great Indifference]
Yes, sir; about five months ago—Is it not, Mr. Solus? You keep account of such things better than I do.

MR SOLUS
Oh! ask me no questions about your wife, Sir Robert; if she had been mine, I would have had her to this moment.

MR PLACID

What, wrested her from the gripe of death?

SIR ROBERT

No, sir; only from the gripe of the Scotch lawyers.

MR SOLUS

More shame for you. Shame to wish to be divorced from a virtuous wife.

MR PLACID

Was that the case? Divorced from a virtuous wife! I never heard of such a circumstance before. Pray, Sir Robert—

[Very anxiously]

—will you indulge me, by letting me know in what manner you were able to bring about so great an event?

SIR ROBERT

It may appear strange to you, sir; but my wife and I did not live happy together.

MR PLACID

Not at all strange, sir: I can conceive—I can conceive very well.

MR SOLUS

Yes, he can conceive that part to perfection.

SIR ROBERT

And so, I was determined on a divorce.

MR PLACID

But then her character could not be unimpeached.

SIR ROBERT

Yes, it was, sir. You must know, we were married in Scotland, and by the laws there, a wife can divorce her husband for breach of fidelity; and so, though my wife's character was unimpeached, mine was not—and she divorced me.

MR PLACID

Is this the law in Scotland?

MR SOLUS

It is. Blessed, blessed, country! that will bind young people together before the years of discretion, and, as soon as they have discretion to repent, will unbind them again!

MR PLACID

I wish I had been married in Scotland.

MR SOLUS

But, Sir Robert, with all this boasting, you must own that your divorce has greatly diminished your fortune.

SIR ROBERT
Mr. Solus, you have frequently hinted at my fortune being impaired; but I do not approve of such notions being received abroad.

MR SOLUS
I beg your pardon: but every body knows that you have played very deep lately, and have been a great loser: and every body knows—

SIR ROBERT
No, sir, every body does not know it, for I contradict the report wherever I go. A man of fashion does not like to be reckoned poor, no more than he likes to be reckoned unhappy. We none of us endeavour to be happy, sir, but merely to be thought so; and for my part, I had rather be in a state of misery, and envied for my supposed happiness, than in a state of happiness, and pitied for my supposed misery.

MR SOLUS
But, consider, these misfortunes, which I have just hinted at, are not of any serious nature, only such as a few years economy—

SIR ROBERT
But, were my wife and her guardian to become acquainted with these little misfortunes, they would triumph in my embarrassments.

MR SOLUS
Lady Ramble triumph!

[They join **MR PLACID**.

She, who was so firmly attached to you, that I believe nothing but a compliance with your repeated request to be separated, caused her to take the step she did.

SIR ROBERT
Yes, I believe she did it to oblige me, and I am very much obliged to her.

MR SOLUS
As good a woman, Mr. Placid—

SIR ROBERT
Very good—but very ugly.

MR SOLUS
She is beautiful.

SIR ROBERT [To **MR SOLUS**]
I tell you, sir, she is hideous. And then she was grown so insufferably peevish.

MR SOLUS
I never saw her out of temper.

SIR ROBERT
Mr. Solus, it is very uncivil of you to praise her before my face. Lady Ramble, at the time I parted with her, had every possible fault both of mind and person, and so I made love to other women in her presence; told her bluntly, that I was tired of her; that I was very sorry to make her uneasy, but that I could not love her any longer.—And was not that frank and open?

MR SOLUS
Oh that I had but such a wife as she was!

SIR ROBERT
I must own I loved her myself when she was young.

MR SOLUS
Do you call her old?

SIR ROBERT
In years I am certainly older than she, but the difference of sex makes her a great deal older than I am. For instance, Mr. Solus, you have often lamented not being married in your youth; but if you had, what would you have now done with an old wife, a woman of your own age?

MR SOLUS
Loved and cherished her.

SIR ROBERT
What, in spite of her loss of beauty?

MR SOLUS
When she had lost her beauty, most likely I should have lost my eyesight, and have been blind to the wane of her charms.

MR PLACID [Anxiously]
But, Sir Robert, you were explaining to me—Mr. Solus, give me leave to speak to Sir Robert—I feel myself particularly interested on this subject.—And, sir, you were explaining to me—

SIR ROBERT
Very true: Where did I leave off? Oh! at my ill usage of my Lady Ramble. Yes, I did use her very ill, and yet she loved me. Many a time, when she has said to me,—"Sir Robert, I detest your principles, your manners, and even your person,"—often at that very instant, I have seen a little sparkle of a wish, peep out of the corner of one eye, that has called out to me, "Oh! Sir Robert, how I long to make it up with you!"

MR SOLUS [To **MR PLACID**]
Do not you wish that your wife had such a little sparkle at the corner of one of her eyes?

SIR ROBERT [To **MR PLACID**]

Sir, do you wish to be divorced?

MR PLACID
I have no such prospect. Mrs. Placid is faithful, and I was married in England.

SIR ROBERT
But if you have an unconquerable desire to part, a separate maintenance will answer nearly the same end—for if your lady and you will only lay down the plan of separation, and agree—

MR PLACID
But, unfortunately, we never do agree!

SIR ROBERT
Then speak of parting, as a thing you dread worse than death; and make it your daily prayer to her, that she will never think of going from you—She will determine upon it directly.

MR PLACID
I thank you; I am very much obliged to you: I thank you a thousand times.

SIR ROBERT
Yes, I have studied the art of teasing a wife; and there is nothing vexes her so much as laughing at her. Can you laugh, Mr. Placid?

MR PLACID
I don't know whether I can; I have not laughed since I married.—But I thank you, sir, for your instructions—I sincerely thank you.

MR SOLUS
And now, Sir Robert, you have had the good-nature to teach this gentleman how to get rid of his wife, will you have the kindness to teach me how to procure one?

[Enter **MR IRWIN**.

SIR ROBERT
Hah! sure I know that gentleman's face?

MR SOLUS
My nephew! Let me escape his solicitations.
[Aside]
—Here, waiter!

[Exit.

MR PLACID
Irwin!
[Starting]
Having sent him a denial, I am ashamed to see him.
[Aside]

Here, Mr. Solus!—

[Exit, following **MR SOLUS**.

MR IRWIN [Aside]
More cool faces! My necessitous visage clears even a club-room.

SIR ROBERT
My dear Captain Irwin, is it you? Yes, 'faith it is—After a nine years' absence, I most sincerely rejoice to see you.

MR IRWIN
Sir Robert, you shake hands with a cordiality I have not experienced these many days, and I thank you.

SIR ROBERT
But what's the matter? You seem to droop—Where have you left your usual spirits? has absence from your country changed your manners?

MR IRWIN
No, sir; but I find some of my countrymen changed. I fancy them less warm, less friendly, than they were; and it is that which, perhaps, has this effect upon me.

SIR ROBERT
Am I changed?

MR IRWIN
You appear an exception.

SIR ROBERT
And I assure you, that instead of being more gloomy, I am even more gay than I was seven years ago; for then, I was upon the point of matrimony—but now, I am just relieved from its cares.

MR IRWIN
I have heard so. But I hope you have not taken so great an aversion to the marriage state as never to marry again?

SIR ROBERT
Perhaps not: But then it must be to some rich heiress.

MR IRWIN
You are right to pay respect to fortune. Money is a necessary article in the marriage contract.

SIR ROBERT
As to that—that would be no great object at present. No, thank Heaven, my estates are pretty large; I have no children; I have a rich uncle, excellent health, admirable spirits;—and thus happy, it would be very strange if I did not meet my old friends with those smiles which never for a moment quit my countenance.

MR IRWIN [Sighing]
In the dispensation of the gifts of Providence, how few are blest like you!

SIR ROBERT
And I assure you, my dear Mr. Irwin, it gives me the most serious reflections, and the most sincere concern, that the bulk of mankind are not.

MR IRWIN
I thank you, sir, most heartily: I thank you for mankind in general, and for myself in particular. For after this generous, unaffected declaration (with less scruple than I should to any one in the world) I will own to you—that I am at this very time in the utmost want of an act of friendship.

SIR ROBERT [Aside]
And so am I—Now must I confess myself a poor man; or pass for an unfeeling one; and I will chuse the latter.

[Bowing with great Ceremony and Coldness.

Any thing that I can command, is at your service.

MR IRWIN [Confounded, and hesitating]
Why, then, Sir Robert—I am almost ashamed to say it—but circumstances have been rather unfavourable.—My wife's father—
[Affecting to smile]
—is not reconciled to us yet—My regiment is broke—My uncle will not part with a farthing.—Lady Eleanor, my wife,—
[Wipes his Eyes]
—has been supported as yet, with some little degree of tenderness, elegance; and—in short, I owe a small sum, which I am afraid of being troubled for; I want a trifle also for our immediate use, and if you would lend me a hundred pounds—though, upon my honour, I am not in a situation to fix the exact time when I can pay it—

SIR ROBERT
My dear sir, never trouble yourself about the time of paying it, because it happens not to be in my power to lend it you.

MR IRWIN
Not in your power! I beg your pardon; but have not you this moment been saying, you are rich?

SIR ROBERT
And is it not very common to be rich without money? Are not half the town rich! And yet half the town has no money. I speak for this end of the town, the west end. The Squares, for instance, part of Piccadilly, down St. James's Street, and so home by Pall Mall. We have all, estates, bonds, drafts, and notes of hand without number; but as for money, we have no such thing belonging to us.

MR IRWIN

I sincerely beg your pardon. And be assured, sir, nothing should have induced me to have taken the liberty I have done, but the misfortunes of my unhappy family, and having understood by your own words, that you were in affluence.

SIR ROBERT

I am in affluence, I am, I am; but not in so much, perhaps, as my hasty, inconsiderate account may have given you reason to believe. I forgot to mention several heavy incumbrances, which you will perceive are great drawbacks on my income.—As my wife sued for the divorce, I have her fortune to return; I have also two sisters to portion off—a circumstance I totally forgot. But, my good friend, though I am not in circumstances to do what you require, I will do something that shall be better. I'll wait upon your father-in-law, (Lord Norland) and entreat him to forgive his daughter: and I am sure he will if I ask him.

MR IRWIN

Impossible.

SIR ROBERT

And so it is, now I recollect: for he is the guardian of my late wife, and a request from me will be received worse than from any other person.—However, Mr. Irwin, depend upon it, that whenever I have an opportunity of serving you, I will. And whenever you shall do me the favour to call upon me, I shall be heartily glad to see you. If I am not at home, you can leave your card, which, you know, is all the same; and depend upon it, I shall be extremely glad to see you, or that, at any time.

[Exit.

MR IRWIN

Is this my native country? Is this the hospitable land which we describe to strangers? No—We are savages to each other; nay, worse—The savage makes his fellow-savage welcome; divides with him his homely fare; gives him the best apartment his hut affords, and tries to hush those griefs that are confided to his bosom—While in this civilized city, among my own countrymen, even among my brother officers in the army, and many of my nearest relations, so very civilized they are, I could not take the liberty to enter under one roof, without a ceremonious invitation,—and that they will not give me. I may leave my card at their door, but as for me, or any one of mine, they would not give us a dinner; unless, indeed, it was in such a style, that we might behold with admiration their grandeur, and return still more depressed to our own poverty.—Can I bear this treatment longer? No, not even for you, my Eleanor. And this—

[Takes out a Pistol.

—shall now be the only friend to whom I will apply—And yet I want the courage to be a villain.

[Enter **MR HARMONY**, speaking as he enters.—**MR IRWIN** conceals the Pistol instantly.

MR HARMONY

Let me see half a dozen newspapers—every paper of the day.

[Enter **WAITER**.

WAITER

That is about three dozen, sir.

MR HARMONY
Get a couple of porters, and bring them all.

[He sits down; they bring him Papers, and he reads—**MR IRWIN** starts, sits down, leans his Head on one of the Tables, and shows various Signs of Uneasiness; then comes forward.

MR IRWIN
Am I a man, a soldier?—And a coward? Yes, I run away, I turn my back on life—I forsake the post, which my commander, Providence, has allotted me, and fly before a banditti of rude misfortunes. Rally me love, connubial and parental love, rally me back to the charge! No, those very affections sound the retreat.

[Sits down with the same Emotions of Distraction as before.

MR HARMONY
That gentleman does not seem happy. I wish I had an opportunity of speaking to him.

[Aside.

MR IRWIN [Coming forward, and speaking again]
But Oh, my wife! what will be your sufferings, when I am brought home to your wretched abode!—And by my own hand!

MR HARMONY
I am afraid, sir, I engross all the news here.

[Holding up the Papers.

MR IRWIN [Still apart]
Poor soul, how her heart will be torn!

MR HARMONY [After looking stedfastly on him]
Captain Irwin, till this moment I had not the pleasure of recollecting you!—It is Mr. Irwin, is it not?

MR IRWIN [His Mind deranged by his Misfortunes]
Yes, sir: but what have you to say to him, more than to a stranger?

MR HARMONY
Nothing more, sir, than to apologize to you, for having addressed you just now in so familiar a manner, before I knew who you were; and to assure you, that although I have no other knowledge of you than from report, and having been once, I believe, in your company at this very house, before you left England; yet, any services of mine, as far as my abilities can reach, you may freely command.

MR IRWIN
Pray, sir, do you live at the west end of the town?

MR HARMONY

I do.

MR IRWIN

Then, sir, your services can be of no use to me.

MR HARMONY

Here is the place where I live, here is my card.

[Gives it to him.

MR IRWIN

And here is mine. And now I presume we have exchanged every act of friendship, which the strict forms of etiquette, in this town, will admit of.

MR HARMONY

By no means, sir. I assure you my professions never go beyond my intentions; and if there is any thing that I can serve you in—

MR IRWIN

Have you no sisters to portion off? no lady's fortune to return? Or, perhaps, you will speak to my wife's father, and entreat him to forgive his child.

MR HARMONY

On that subject, you may command me; for I have the honour to be intimately acquainted with Lord Norland.

MR IRWIN

But is there no reason you may recollect, why you would be the most unfit person in the world to apply to him?

MR HARMONY

None. I have been honoured with marks of his friendship for many years past: and I do not know any one who could, with less hazard of his resentment, venture to name his daughter to him.

MR IRWIN

Well, sir, if you should see him two or three days hence—when I am set out on a journey I am going—if you will then say a kind word to him for my wife and children, I'll thank you.

MR HARMONY

I will go to him instantly.

[Going.

MR IRWIN

No, do not see him yet; stay till I am gone. He will do nothing till I am gone.

MR HARMONY

May I ask where you are going?

MR IRWIN
No very tedious journey; but it is a country, to those who go without a proper passport, always fatal.

MR HARMONY
I'll see Lord Norland to-night: perhaps I may persuade him to prevent your journey. I'll see him to-night, or early in the morning, depend upon it.—I am a man of my word, sir, though I must own I do live at the west end of the town.

[Exit.

MR IRWIN
'Sdeath! am I become the ridicule of my fellow-creatures! or am I not in my senses?—I know this is London—this house a tavern—I know I have a wife—Oh! 'twere better to be mad than to remember her!—She has a father—he is rich and proud—that I will not forget. But I will pass his house, and send a malediction as I pass it.
[Furiously]
No; breathe out my last sigh at his inhospitable door, and that sigh shall breathe—forgiveness.

[Exit.

SCENE II

The Lodgings of Mr. Irwin

Enter **MRS PLACID**, followed by **LADY ELEANOR IRWIN**.

LADY ELEANOR
I am ashamed of the trouble I have given you, Mrs. Placid. It had been sufficient to have sent me home in your carriage; to attend me yourself was ceremonious.

MRS PLACID
My dear Lady Eleanor, I was resolved to come home with you, as soon as Mr. Placid desired I would not.

LADY ELEANOR
Was that the cause of your politeness? I am sorry it should.

MRS PLACID
Why sorry? It is not proper he should have his way in every thing.

LADY ELEANOR
But I am afraid you seldom let him have it at all.

MRS PLACID
Yes, I do.—But where, my dear, is Mr. Irwin?

LADY ELEANOR [Weeping]
I cannot hear the name of Mr. Irwin, without shedding tears: his health has so declined of late, and his spirits been so bad—sometimes I even fear for a failure in his mind.

[Weeps again.

MRS PLACID
Is not he at home?

LADY ELEANOR
I hope he is.

[Goes to the Side of the Scenes.

Tell your master, Mrs. Placid is here.

[Enter a **SERVANT**.

SERVANT
My master is not come in yet, madam.

LADY ELEANOR
Not yet? I am very sorry for it;—very sorry indeed.

MRS PLACID
Bless me, my dear, don't look thus pale. Come, sit down, and I'll stay with you till he returns.

[Sits down herself.

LADY ELEANOR
My dear, you forget, that Mr. Placid is in the carriage at the door all this time.

MRS PLACID
No, I don't.—Come, let us sit and have half an hour's conversation.

LADY ELEANOR
Nay, I insist upon your going to him, or desiring him to walk in.

MRS PLACID
Now I think of it, they may as well drive him home, and come back for me.

[Enter **MR PLACID**.

Why, surely, Mr. Placid, you were very impatient!—I think you might have waited a few minutes longer.

MR PLACID
I would have waited, my dear, but the evening is so damp.

LADY ELEANOR

Ah! 'tis this evening—that makes me alarmed for Mr. Irwin.

MR PLACID

Lady Eleanor, you are one of the most tender, anxious, and affectionate wives, I ever knew.

MRS PLACID

There! Now he wishes he was your husband—he admires the conduct of every wife but his own, and envies every married man of his acquaintance. But it is very ungenerous in you.

MR PLACID

So it is, my dear, and not at all consistent with the law of equity; for I am sure, there is not one of my acquaintance who envies me.

MRS PLACID

Mr. Placid, your behaviour throughout this whole day, has been so totally different from what it ever was before, that I am half resolved to live no longer with you.

MR PLACID [Aside]

It will do—It will do.

LADY ELEANOR

Oh, my dear friends, do not talk of parting:—how can you, while every blessing smiles on your union? Even I, who have reason to regret mine, yet, while that load of grief, a separation from Mr. Irwin, is but averted, I will think every other affliction supportable.

[A loud Rapping at the Door.

That is he!

MRS PLACID

Why, you seem in raptures at his return.

LADY ELEANOR

I know no greater rapture.

[Enter **MR IRWIN**, pale, trembling, and disordered.

My dear, you are not well, I see.

MR IRWIN [Aside to her in Anger]

Why do you speak of it?

MR PLACID

How do you do, Irwin?

MR IRWIN

I am glad to see you.

[Bows.

MRS PLACID
But I am sorry to see you look so ill.

MR IRWIN
I have only been taking a glass too much.

[**LADY ELEANOR** weeps.

MR PLACID
Pshaw! Don't I know you never drink.

MR IRWIN
You are mistaken—I do, when my wife is not by. I am afraid of her.

MR PLACID
Impossible.

MR IRWIN
What! to be afraid of one's wife?

MR PLACID
No, I think that very possible.

MRS PLACID
But it does not look well when it is so; it makes a man appear contemptible, and a woman a termagant. Come, Mr. Placid, I cannot stay another moment. Good night. Heaven bless you!
[To **LADY ELEANOR**]
—Good night, my dear Mr. Irwin;—and now, pray take my advice, and keep up your spirits.

MR IRWIN
I will, madam.—

[Shaking Hands with **MR PLACID**.

And do you keep up your spirits.

[Exeunt **MR** and **MRS PLACID**.—**MR IRWIN** shuts the Door with Care after them, and looks round the Room, as if he feared to be seen or overheard.

I am glad they are gone.—I spoke unkindly to you just now, did I not? My temper is altered lately; and yet I love you.

LADY ELEANOR
I never doubted it, nor ever will.

MR IRWIN
If you did, you would wrong me; for there is no danger I would not risk for your sake: there is not an infamy I would not be branded with, to make you happy, nor a punishment I would not undergo, with joy, for your welfare.—But there's a bar to this; we are unfortunately so entwined together, so linked, so rivetted, so cruelly, painfully fettered, to each other, you could not be happy unless I shared the selfsame happiness with you.—But you will learn better—now you are in London, and amongst fashionable wives; you must learn better.

[Walks about, and smiles, with a ghastly Countenance.

LADY ELEANOR
Do not talk, do not look thus wildly—Indeed, indeed, you make me very uneasy.

MR IRWIN
What! uneasy when I come to bring you comfort; and such comfort as you have not experienced for many a day?

[He pulls out a Pocketbook.

Here is a friend in our necessity,—a friend, that brings a thousand friends; plenty and—no, not always—peace.

[He takes several Papers from the Book, and puts them into her Hands—She looks at them, then screams.

LADY ELEANOR
Ah! 'tis money!

[Trembling.

These are bank notes!

MR IRWIN
Hush! for Heaven's sake, hush! We shall be discovered.

[Trembling, and in great Perturbation.

What alarms you thus?

LADY ELEANOR
What alarms you?

MR IRWIN
Do you say, I am frightened?

LADY ELEANOR
A sight so new, has frightened me.

MR IRWIN

Nay, they are your own: by Heaven, they are! No one on earth has a better, or a fairer right to them than yourself. It was a laudable act, by which I obtained them.—The parent bird had forsook its young, and I but forced it back, to perform the rites of nature.

LADY ELEANOR

You are insane, I fear. No, no, I do not fear—I hope you are.

[A loud Rapping at the Street Door—He starts, takes the Notes from her, and puts them hastily into his Pocket.

MR IRWIN

Go to the door yourself; and if 'tis any one who asks for me, say, I am not come home yet.

[She goes out, then returns.

LADY ELEANOR

It is the person belonging to the house; no one to us.

MR IRWIN

My dear Eleanor, are you willing to quit London with me in about two hours time?

LADY ELEANOR

Instantly.

MR IRWIN

Nay, not only London, but England.

LADY ELEANOR

This world, if you desire it. To go in company with you, will make the journey pleasant; and all I loved on earth would still be with me.

MR IRWIN

You can, then, leave your father without regret, never, never, to see him more?

LADY ELEANOR

Why should I think on him, who will not think on me?

[Weeps.

MR IRWIN

But our children—

LADY ELEANOR

We are not to leave them?

MR IRWIN

One of them we must: but do not let that give you uneasiness. You know he has never lived with us since his infancy, and cannot pine for the loss of parents, whom he has never known.

LADY ELEANOR
But I have known him. He was my first; and, sometimes, I think, more closely wound around my heart, then all the rest. The grief I felt on being forced to leave him, when we went abroad, and the constant anxiety I have since experienced, lest he should not be kindly treated, have augmented, I think, my tenderness.

MR IRWIN
All my endeavours to-day, as well as every other day, have been in vain, to find into what part of the country his nurse has taken him.—Nay, be not thus overcome with tears; we will (in spite of all my haste to begone) stay one more miserable day here, in hopes to procure intelligence, so as to take him with us; and then—smile with contempt on all we leave behind.

[Exeunt.

ACT THE THIRD

SCENE I

A Library at Lord Norland's

Enter **LORD NORLAND**, followed by **MR HARMONY**.

LORD NORLAND [In Anger]
I tell you, Mr. Harmony, that if an indifferent person, one on whom I had never bestowed a favour in my life, were to offend me, it is in my nature never to forgive. Can I then forgive my own daughter, my only child, on whom I heaped continual marks of the most affectionate fondness? Shall she dare to offend me in the tenderest point, and you dare to suppose I will pardon her?

MR HARMONY
Your child, consider.

LORD NORLAND
The weakest argument you can use. As my child, was she not most bound to obey me? As my child, ought she not to have sacrificed her own happiness to mine? Instead of which, mine has been yielded up for a whim, a fancy, a fancy to marry a beggar; and, as such is her choice, let her beg with him.

MR HARMONY
She does, by me;—pleads hard for your forgiveness.

LORD NORLAND
If I thought she dared to send a message to me, though dictated on her knees, she should find, that she had not yet felt the full force of my resentment.

MR HARMONY
What could you do more?

LORD NORLAND
I have done nothing yet. At present, I have only abandoned her;—but I can persecute.

MR HARMONY
I have no doubt of it: and, that I may not be the means of aggravating your displeasure, I assure you, that what I have now said has been entirely from myself, without any desire of hers; and, at the same time, I give you my promise, I will never presume to introduce the subject again.

LORD NORLAND
On this condition (but on no other) I forgive you now.

MR HARMONY
And now, then, my lord, let us pass from those who have forfeited your love, to those who possess it.—I heard, sometime ago, but I never felt myself disposed to mention it to you, that you had adopted a young man as your son.

LORD NORLAND
A young man! Pshaw! No; a boy—a mere child, who fell in my way by accident.

MR HARMONY
A chance child!—Ho! ho! I understand you.

LORD NORLAND
Do not jest with me, sir. Do I look—

MR HARMONY
Yes, you look as if you would be ashamed to own it, if you had one.

LORD NORLAND
But this boy I am not ashamed of: he is a favourite—rather a favourite. I did not like him so well at first;—but custom,—and having a poor creature entirely at one's mercy, one begins to love it merely from the idea of—What would be its fate if one did not?

MR HARMONY
Is he an orphan, then?

LORD NORLAND
No.

MR HARMONY
You have a friendship for his parents?

LORD NORLAND [Sighing]
I never saw the father: his mother I had a friendship for once.

MR HARMONY
Ay, while the husband was away?

LORD NORLAND
I tell you, no.
[Violently]
—But ask no more questions. Who his parents are, is a secret, which neither he, nor any one (that is now living) knows, except myself; nor ever shall.

MR HARMONY
Well, my lord, since 'tis your pleasure to consider him as your child, I sincerely wish you may experience more duty from him, than you have done from your daughter.

LORD NORLAND
Thank Heaven, his disposition is not in the least like hers—No:
[Very much impassioned]
I have the joy to say, that never child was so unlike its mother.

MR HARMONY [Starting]
How! his mother!

LORD NORLAND
Confusion!—what have I said?—I am ashamed—

MR HARMONY
No,—be proud.

LORD NORLAND
Of what?

MR HARMONY
That you have a lawful heir to all your riches; proud, that you have a grandson.

LORD NORLAND
I would have concealed it from all the world; I wished it even unknown to myself. And, let me tell you, sir, (as not by my design, but through my inadvertency, you are become acquainted with this secret) that, if ever you breathe it to a single creature, the boy shall answer for it; for, were he known to be hers, though he were dearer to me than ever she was, I would turn him from my house, and cast him from my heart, as I have done her.

MR HARMONY
I believe you;—and, in compassion to the child, give you my solemn promise, never to reveal who he is. I have heard that those unfortunate parents left an infant behind when they went abroad, and that they now lament him as lost. Will you satisfy my curiosity, in what manner you sought and found him out?

LORD NORLAND
Do you suppose I searched for him? No;—he was forced upon me. A woman followed me, about eight years ago, in the fields adjoining to my country seat, with a half-starved boy in her hand, and asked my

charity for my grandchild: the impression of the word made me turn round involuntarily; and, casting my eyes upon him, I was rejoiced not to find a feature of his mother's in all his face; and I began to feel something like pity for him. In short, he caught such fast hold by one of my fingers, that I asked him, carelessly, "if he would go home and live with me?" On which, he answered me so willingly, "Yes," I took him at his word.

MR HARMONY
And did never your regard for him, plead in his mother's behalf?

LORD NORLAND
Never:—for, by Heaven, I would as soon forgive the robber, who met me last night at my own door, and, holding a pistol to my breast, took from me a sum to a considerable amount, as I would pardon her.

MR HARMONY
Did such an accident happen to you?

LORD NORLAND
Have you not heard of it?

MR HARMONY
No.

LORD NORLAND
It is amazing we cannot put a stop to such depredations.

MR HARMONY
Provisions are so scarce!

[Enter a **SERVANT**.

SERVANT
Miss Wooburn, my lord, if you are not engaged, will come and sit an hour with you.

LORD NORLAND
I have no company but such as she is perfectly acquainted with, and I shall be glad of her visit.

[Exit **SERVANT**.

MR HARMONY
You forget I am a stranger, and my presence may not be welcome.

LORD NORLAND
A stranger! What, to my ward? to Lady Ramble? for that is the name which custom would authorize her to keep; but such courtesy she disdains, in contempt of the unworthy giver of the title.

MR HARMONY
I am intimate with Sir Robert, my lord: and, though I acknowledge that both you and his late wife have cause for complaint,—yet Sir Robert has still many virtues.

LORD NORLAND

Not one. He is the most vile, the most detestable of characters. He not only contradicted my will in the whole of his conduct, but he seldom met me that he did not give me some personal affront.

MR HARMONY

It is, however, generally held better to be uncivil in a person's presence, than in his absence.

LORD NORLAND

He was uncivil to me in every respect.

MR HARMONY

That I will deny; for I have heard Sir Robert, in your absence, say such things in your favour!—

LORD NORLAND

Indeed!

MR HARMONY

Most assuredly.

LORD NORLAND

I wish he had sometimes done me the honour to have spoken politely to my face.

MR HARMONY

That is not Sir Robert's way;—he is no flatterer. But then, no sooner has your back been turned, than I have heard him lavish in your praise.

LORD NORLAND

I must own, Mr. Harmony, that I never looked upon Sir Robert as incorrigible. I could always discern a ray of understanding, and a beam of virtue, through all his foibles; nor would I have urged the divorce, but that I found his wife's sensibility could not bear his neglect; and, even now, notwithstanding her endeavour to conceal it, she pines in secret, and laments her hard fortune. All my hopes of restoring her health rest on one prospect—that of finding a man worthy my recommendation for her second husband, and, by thus creating a second passion, expel the first.—Mr. Harmony, you and I have been long acquainted—I have known your disposition from your infancy—Now, if such a man as you were to offer—

MR HARMONY

You flatter me.

LORD NORLAND

I do not—would you venture to become her husband?

MR HARMONY

I cannot say, I have any particular desire;—but if it will oblige either you or her,—for my part, I think the short time we live in this world, we should do all we can to oblige each other.

LORD NORLAND

I should rejoice at such an union myself, and, I think, I can answer for her.—You permit me, then, to make overtures to her in your name?

MR HARMONY [Considering]
This is rather a serious business—However, I never did make a difficulty, when I wished to oblige a friend.—But there is one proviso, my lord; I must first mention it to Sir Robert.

LORD NORLAND
Why so?

MR HARMONY
Because he and I have always been very intimate friends: and to marry his wife without even telling him of it, will appear very uncivil!

LORD NORLAND
Do you mean, then, to ask his consent?

MR HARMONY
Not absolutely his consent; but I will insinuate the subject to him, and obtain his approbation in a manner suitable to my own satisfaction.

LORD NORLAND
You will oblige me, then, if you will see him as early as possible; for it is reported he is going abroad.

MR HARMONY
I will go to him immediately;—and, my lord, I will do all in my power to oblige you. Sir Robert, and the lady—[Aside] but as to obliging myself, that was never one of my considerations.

[Exit.

[Enter **MISS WOOBURN**.

LORD NORLAND
I am sorry to see you thus; you have been weeping! Will you still lament your separation from a cruel husband, as if you had followed a kind one to the grave?

MISS WOOBURN
By no means, my lord. Tears from our sex are not always the result of grief; they are frequently no more than little sympathetic tributes, which we pay to our fellow beings, while the mind and the heart are steeled against the weakness, which our eyes indicate.

LORD NORLAND
Can you say, your mind and heart are so steeled?

MISS WOOBURN
I can: My mind is as firmly fixed against Sir Robert Ramble, as, at our first acquaintance, it was fixed upon him. And I solemnly protest—

LORD NORLAND

To a man of my age and observation, protestations are vain.—Give me a proof, that you have rooted him from your heart.

MISS WOOBURN

Any proof you require, I will give you without a moment's hesitation.

LORD NORLAND

I take you at your word; and desire you to accept a gentleman, whom I shall recommend for your second husband.

[**MISS WOOBURN** starts.

—You said, you would not hesitate a moment.

MISS WOOBURN

I thought I should not;—but this is something so unexpected—

LORD NORLAND

You break your word, then; and still give cause for this ungrateful man to ridicule your fondness for him.

MISS WOOBURN

No, I will put an end to that humiliation; and whoever the gentleman is whom you mean to propose— Yet, do not name him at present—but give me the satisfaction of keeping the promise I have made to you (at least for a little time) without exactly knowing how far it extends; for, in return I have a promise to ask from you, before I acquaint you with the nature of your engagement.

LORD NORLAND

I give my promise. Now name your request.

MISS WOOBURN

Then, my lord—
[Hesitating, and confused]
—the law gave me back, upon my divorce from Sir Robert, the very large fortune which I brought to him.—I am afraid, that, in his present circumstances, to enforce the strict payment of this debt would very much embarrass him.

LORD NORLAND

What if it did?

MISS WOOBURN

It is my entreaty to you (in whose hands is invested the power to demand this right of law) to lay my claim aside for the present.

[**LORD NORLAND** offers to speak.

I know, my lord, what you are going to say; I know Sir Robert is not now, but I can never forget that he has been, my husband.

LORD NORLAND
To show my gratitude for your compliance with the request I have just made you,

[Goes to a Table in the Library.

—here is the bond by which I am empowered to seize on the greatest part of his estates in right of you: take the bond into your own possession, till your next husband demands it of you; and, by the time you have called him husband for a few weeks, this tenderness, or delicacy, to Sir Robert, will be worn away.

[Enter **MR HARMONY**, hastily.

MR HARMONY
My lord, I beg pardon; but I forgot to mention—

MISS WOOBURN
Oh, Mr. Harmony, I have not seen you before, I know not when: I am particularly happy at your calling just now, for I have—
[Hesitating]
—a little favour to ask of you.

MR HARMONY
If it were a great favour, madam, you might command me.

MISS WOOBURN
But—my lord, I beg your pardon—the favour I have to ask of Mr. Harmony must be told to him in private.

LORD NORLAND
Oh! I am sure I have not the least objection to you and Mr. Harmony having a private conference. I'll leave you together.

[**MR HARMONY** appears embarrassed.

You do not derange my business—I'll be back in a short time.

[Exit.

MISS WOOBURN
Mr. Harmony, you are the very man on earth whom I most wanted to see.
[To **MR HARMONY**]
I know the kindness of your heart, the liberality of your sentiments, and I wish to repose a charge to your trust, very near to me indeed—but you must be secret.

MR HARMONY
When a lady reposes a trust in me, I shouldn't be a man if I were not.

MISS WOOBURN

I must first inform you, that Lord Norland has just drawn from me a promise, that I will once more enter into the marriage state: and without knowing to whom he intends to give me, I will keep my promise. But it is in vain to say, that though I mean all duty and fidelity to my second husband, I shall not experience moments when my thoughts—will wander on my first.

MR HARMONY [Starting]
Hem!—Hem!—
[To her]
—Indeed!

MISS WOOBURN
I must always rejoice in Sir Robert's successes, and lament over his misfortunes.

MR HARMONY
If that is all—

MISS WOOBURN
No, I would go one step further:

[**MR HARMONY** starts again.

I would secure him from those distresses, which to hear of, will disturb my peace of mind. I know his fortune has suffered very much, and I cannot, will not, place it in the power of the man, whom my Lord Norland may point out for my next marriage, to harass him farther—This is the writing, by which that gentleman may claim the part of my fortune from Sir Robert Ramble, which is in landed property; carry it, my dear Mr. Harmony, to Sir Robert instantly; and tell him—that, in separating from him, I meant only to give him liberty, not make him the debtor, perhaps the prisoner, of my future husband.

MR HARMONY
Madam, I will most undoubtedly take this bond to my friend; but will you give me leave to suggest to you,—that the person on whom you bestow your hand may be a little surprised to find, that while he is in possession of you, Sir Robert is in the possession of your fortune.

MISS WOOBURN
Do not imagine, sir, that I shall marry any man, without first declaring what I have done—I only wish at present it should be concealed from Lord Norland—When this paper is given, as I have required, it cannot be recalled: and when that is past, I shall divulge my conduct to whom I please: and first of all, to him, who shall offer me his addresses.

MR HARMONY
And if he is a man of my feelings, his addresses will be doubly importunate for this proof of liberality to your former husband.—But are you sure, that, in the return of this bond, there is no secret affection, no latent spark of love?

MISS WOOBURN
None, I know my heart; and if there was, I could not ask you, Mr. Harmony (nor any one like you), to be the messenger of an imprudent passion. Sir Robert's vanity, I know, may cause him to judge otherwise;

but undeceive him; let him know, this is a sacrifice to the golden principles of duty, and not an offering to the tinselled shrine of love.

[Enter **LORD NORLAND**.

MISS WOOBURN
Put up the bond.—

[**MR HARMONY** conceals it.

LORD NORLAND
Well, my dear, have you made your request?

MISS WOOBURN
Yes, my lord.

LORD NORLAND
And has he granted it?

MR HARMONY
Yes, my lord. I am going to grant it.

LORD NORLAND
I sincerely wish you both joy of this good understanding between you. But, Mr. Harmony,—
[In a Whisper]
—are not you going to Sir Robert?

MR HARMONY
Yes, my lord, I am going this moment.

LORD NORLAND
Make haste, then, and do not forget your errand.

MR HARMONY
No, my lord, I sha'n't forget my errand: it won't slip my memory—Good morning, my lord:—good morning, madam.

[Exit.

LORD NORLAND
Now, my dear, as you and Mr. Harmony seem to be on such excellent terms, I think I may venture to tell you (if he has not yet told you himself), that he is the man, who is to be your husband.

MISS WOOBURN
He! Mr. Harmony!—No, my lord, he has not told me; and I am confident he never will.

LORD NORLAND
What makes you think so?

MISS WOOBURN

Because—because—he must be sensible he would not be the man I should chuse.

LORD NORLAND

And where is the woman who marries the man she would chuse? you are reversing the order of society; men only have the right of choice in marriage. Were women permitted theirs, we should have handsome beggars allied to our noblest families, and no such object in our whole island as an old maid.

MISS WOOBURN

But being denied that choice, why am I forbid to remain as I am?

LORD NORLAND

What are you now? Neither a widow, a maid, nor a wife. If I could fix a term to your present state, I should not be thus anxious to place you in another.

MISS WOOBURN

I am perfectly acquainted with your friendly motives, and feel the full force of your advice.—I therefore renew my promise—and although Mr. Harmony (in respect to the marriage state) is as little to my wishes as any man on earth, I will nevertheless endeavour—whatever struggles it may cost me—to be to him, if he prefers his suit, a dutiful, an obedient—but, for a loving wife, that I can never be again.

[Exeunt severally.

SCENE II

An Apartment at Sir Robert Ramble's

Enter **SIR ROBERT**, and **MR HARMONY**.

SIR ROBERT

I thank you for this visit. I was undetermined what to do with myself. Your company has determined me to stay at home.

MR HARMONY

I was with a gentleman just now, Sir Robert, and you were the subject of our conversation.

SIR ROBERT

Had it been a lady, I should be anxious to know what she said.

MR HARMONY

I have been with a lady, likewise: and she made you the subject of her discourse.

SIR ROBERT

But was she handsome?

MR HARMONY

Very handsome.

SIR ROBERT

My dear fellow, what is her name? What did she say, and where may I meet with her?

MR HARMONY

Her name is Wooburn.

SIR ROBERT

That is the name of my late wife.

MR HARMONY

It is her I mean.

SIR ROBERT

Zounds, you had just put my spirits into a flame, and now you throw cold water all over me.

MR HARMONY

I am sorry to hear you say so, for I came from her this moment;—and what do you think is the present she has given me to deliver to you?

SIR ROBERT

Pshaw! I want no presents. Some of my old love-letters returned, I suppose, to remind me of my inconstancy.

MR HARMONY

Do not undervalue her generosity; this is her present:—this bond, which has power to take from you three thousand a year, her right.

SIR ROBERT

Ah! this is a present, indeed! Are you certain you speak truth? Let me look at it;—Sure my eyes deceive me!—No, by Heaven it is true!
[Reads]
The very thing I wanted, and will make me perfectly happy. Now I'll be generous again; my bills shall be paid, my gaming debts cancelled, poor Irwin shall find a friend; and I'll send Miss Wooburn as pretty a copy of verses as ever I wrote in my life.

MR HARMONY

Take care how you treat with levity a woman of her elevated mind. She charged me to assure you, that love had no share whatever in this act, which is mere compassion to the embarrassed state of your affairs.

SIR ROBERT

Sir, I would have you to know, I am no object of compassion. However, a lady's favour one cannot return; and so I'll keep this thing.

[Puts the Bond in his Pocket.

MR HARMONY

Nay, if your circumstances are different from what she imagines, give it me back, and I will restore it to her.

SIR ROBERT

No, poor thing! it would break her heart to send it back—No, I'll keep it—She would never forgive me, were I to send it back. I'll keep it. And she is welcome to attribute her concern for me to what she pleases. But surely you can see—you can understand—But Heaven bless her for her love! and I would love her in return—if I could.

MR HARMONY

You would not talk thus, if you had seen the firm dignity with which she gave me that paper—"Assure him," said she, "no remaining affection comes along with it, but merely a duty which I owe him, to protect him from the humiliation of being a debtor to the man, whom I am going to marry."

SIR ROBERT [With the utmost Emotion]

Why, she is not going to be married again!

MR HARMONY

I believe so.

SIR ROBERT

But are you sure of it, sir? Are you sure of it?

MR HARMONY

Both she and her guardian told me so.

SIR ROBERT

That guardian, my Lord Norland, is one of the basest, vilest of men.—I tell you what, sir, I'll resent this usage.

MR HARMONY

Wherefore?—As to his being the means of bringing about your separation, in that he obliged you.

SIR ROBERT

Yes, sir, he did, he certainly did;—but though I am not in the least offended with him on that account (for at that I rejoice), yet I will resent his disposing of her a second time.

MR HARMONY

And wherefore?

SIR ROBERT

Because, little regard as I have for her myself, yet no other man shall dare to treat her so ill as I have done.

MR HARMONY

Do not fear it—Her next husband will be a man, who, I can safely say, will never insult, or even offend her; but sooth, indulge, and make her happy.

SIR ROBERT

And do you dare to tell me, that her next husband shall make her happy? Now that is worse than the other—No, sir, no man shall ever have it to say, he has made her either happy or miserable, but myself.

MR HARMONY

I know of but one way to prevent it.

SIR ROBERT

And what is that?

MR HARMONY

Pay your addresses to her, and marry her again yourself.

SIR ROBERT

And I would, rather than she should be happy with any body else.

MR HARMONY

To show that I am wholly disinterested in this affair, I will carry her a letter from you, if you like, and say all I can in your behalf.

SIR ROBERT

Ha! ha! ha! Now, my dear Harmony, you carry your goodnatured simplicity too far. However, I thank you—I sincerely thank you—But do you imagine I should be such a blockhead, as to make love to the same woman I made love to seven years ago, and who for the last six years I totally neglected?

MR HARMONY

Yes; for if you have neglected her six years, she will now be a novelty.

SIR ROBERT

Egad, and so she will. You are right.

MR HARMONY

But being in possession of her fortune, you can be very happy without her.

SIR ROBERT

Take her fortune back, sir.

[Taking the Bond from his Pocket, and offering it to **MR HARMONY**.

I would starve, I would perish, die in poverty, and infamy, rather than owe an obligation to a vile, perfidious, inconstant woman.

MR HARMONY

Consider, Sir Robert, if you insist on my taking this bond back, it may fall into the husband's hands.

SIR ROBERT
Take it back—I insist upon it.

[Gives it him, and **MR HARMONY** puts it up.

But, Mr. Harmony, depend on it, Lord Norland shall hear from me, in the most serious manner, for his interference—I repeat, he is the vilest, the most villanous of men.

MR HARMONY
How can you speak with such rancour of a nobleman, who speaks of you in the highest terms?

SIR ROBERT
Does he, 'faith?

MR HARMONY
He owns you have some faults.

SIR ROBERT
I know I have.

MR HARMONY
But he thinks your good qualities are numberless.

SIR ROBERT
Now, dam'me if ever I thought so ill of him as I have appeared to do!—But who is the intended husband, my dear friend? Tell me, that I may laugh at him, and make you laugh at him.

MR HARMONY
No, I am not inclined to laugh at him.

SIR ROBERT
Is it old Solus?

MR HARMONY
No.

SIR ROBERT
But I will bet you a wager it is somebody equally ridiculous.

MR HARMONY
I never bet.

SIR ROBERT
Solus is mad for a wife, and has been praising mine up to the heavens,—you need say no more—I know it is he.

MR HARMONY

Upon my honour, it is not. However, I cannot disclose to you at present the person's name; I must first obtain Lord Norland's permission.

SIR ROBERT
I shall ask you no more. I'll write to her, she will tell me;—or I'll pay her a visit, and ask her boldly myself.— Do you think—
[Anxiously]
—do you think she would see me!

MR HARMONY
You can but try.

[Enter a **SERVANT**.

SERVANT
Mr. Solus.

SIR ROBERT
Now I will find out the secret immediately.—I'll charge him with being the intended husband.

MR HARMONY
I won't stay to hear you.

[Enter **MR SOLUS**.

Mr. Solus, how do you do? I am extremely sorry that my engagements take me away as soon as you enter.

[Exit **MR HARMONY**, running, to avoid an Explanation.

MR SOLUS
Sir Robert, what is the matter? Has any thing ruffled you? Why, I never saw you look more out of temper, even while you were married.

SIR ROBERT
Ah! that I had never married! never known what marriage was! for, even at this moment, I feel its torments in my heart.

MR SOLUS
I have often heard of the torments of matrimony; but I conceive, that at the worst, they are nothing more than a kind of violent tickling, which will force the tears into your eyes, though at the same time you are bursting your sides with laughter.

SIR ROBERT
You have defined marriage too favourably; there is no laughter in the state; all is melancholy, all gloom.

MR SOLUS

Now I think marriage is an excellent remedy for the spleen. I have known a gentleman at a feast receive an affront, disguise his rage, step home, vent it all upon his wife, return to his companions, and be as good company as if nothing had happened.

SIR ROBERT
But even the necessary expenses of a wife should alarm you.

MR SOLUS
I can then retrench some of my own. Oh! my dear sir, a married man has so many delightful privileges to what a bachelor has;—An old lady will introduce her daughters to you in a dishabille—"It does not signify, my dears, it's a married man"—One lady will suffer you to draw on her glove—"Never mind, it's a married man"—Another will permit you to pull on her slipper; a third will even take you into her bedchamber—"Pshaw, it's nothing but a married man."

SIR ROBERT
But the weight of your fetters will overbalance all these joys.

MR SOLUS
And I cannot say, notwithstanding you are relieved from those fetters, that I see much joy or content here.

SIR ROBERT
I am not very well at present; I have the head ache; and, if ever a wife can be of comfort to her husband, it must be when he is indisposed. A wife, then, binds up your head, mixes your powders, bathes your temples, and hovers about you, in a way that is most endearing.

MR SOLUS
Don't speak of it; I long to have one hover about me. But I will—I am determined I will, before I am a week older. Don't speak, don't attempt to persuade me not. Your description has renewed my eagerness—I will be married.

SIR ROBERT
And without pretending not to know whom you mean to make your choice, I tell you plainly, it is Miss Wooburn, it is my late wife.—I know you have made overtures to my Lord Norland, and that he has given his consent.

MR SOLUS
You tell me a great piece of news—I'll go ask my lord if it be true; and if he says it is, I shall be very glad to find it so.

SIR ROBERT
That is right, sir; marry her, marry her;—I give you joy,—that's all.—Ha! ha! ha! I think I should know her temper.—But if you will venture to marry her, I sincerely wish you happy.

MR SOLUS
And if we are not, you know we can be divorced.

SIR ROBERT

Not always. Take my advice, and live as you are.

MR SOLUS
You almost stagger my resolution.—I had painted such bright prospects in marriage:—Good day to you.
[Going, returns]
—You think I had better not marry?

SIR ROBERT
You are undone if you do.

MR SOLUS [Sighing]
You ought to know from experience.

SIR ROBERT
From that I speak.

MR SOLUS [Going to the Door, and returning once or twice, as undetermined in his Resolution]
But then, what a poor, disconsolate object shall I live, without a wife to hover about me; to bind up my head, and bathe my temples! Oh! I am impatient for all the chartered rights, privileges, and immunities of a married man.

[Exit.

SIR ROBERT
Furies! racks! torments!—I cannot bear what I feel, and yet I am ashamed to own I feel any thing!

[Enter **MR PLACID**.

MR PLACID
My dear Sir Robert, give me joy! Mrs. Placid and I are come to the very point you advised: matters are in the fairest way for a separation.

SIR ROBERT
I do give you joy, and most sincerely.—You are right; you will soon be as happy as I am.
[Sighing]
But, would you suppose it? that deluded woman, my wife, is going to be married again! I thought she had experienced enough from me.

MR PLACID
You are hurt, I see, lest the world should say, she has forgot you.

SIR ROBERT
She cannot forget me; I defy her to forget me.

MR PLACID
Who is her intended husband?

SIR ROBERT

Solus, Solus. An old man—an ugly man. He left me this moment, and owned it—owned it! Go after him, will you, and persuade him not to have her.

MR PLACID
My advice will have no effect, for you know he is determined upon matrimony.

SIR ROBERT
Then could not you, my dear sir (as you are going to be separated,) could not you recommend him to marry your wife?—It will be all the same to him, and I shall like it much better.

MR PLACID
Ours will not be a divorce, consider, but merely a separate maintenance. But were it otherwise, I wish no man so ill, as to wish him married to Mrs. Placid.

SIR ROBERT
That is my case exactly—I wish no man so ill, as to wish him married to my Lady Ramble; and poor old Solus in particular, poor old man! a very good sort of man—I have a great friendship for Solus.—I can't stay a moment in the house—I must go somewhere—I'll go to Solus—No, I'll go to Lord Norland—No, I'll go to Harmony; and then I'll call on you, and we'll take a bottle together; and when you are become free—

[Takes his Hand]

—we'll both join, from that moment we'll join, to laugh at, to contemn, to despise, all those who boast of the joys of conjugal love.

[Exeunt.

ACT THE FOURTH

SCENE I

An Apartment at Mr. Harmony's

Enter **MR HARMONY**.

MR HARMONY
And now for one of the most painful tasks that brotherly love ever draws upon me; to tell another the suit, of which I gave him hope, has failed.—Yet, if I can but overcome Captain Irwin's delicacy so far, as to prevail on him to accept one proof more of my good wishes towards him;—but to a man of his nice sense of obligations, the offer must be made with caution.

[Enter **LORD NORLAND**.

LORD NORLAND

Mr. Harmony, I beg your pardon: I come in thus abruptly, from the anxiety I feel concerning what passed between us this morning in respect to Miss Wooburn. You have not changed your mind, I hope?

MR HARMONY
Indeed, my lord, I am very sorry that it will not be in my power to oblige you.

LORD NORLAND [In Anger]
How, sir? Did not you give me your word?

MR HARMONY
Only conditionally, my lord.

LORD NORLAND
And what were the conditions?

MR HARMONY
Have you forgot them? Her former husband—

[Enter a **SERVANT**.

SERVANT
Sir Robert Ramble is in his carriage at the door, and, if you are at leisure, will come in.

MR HARMONY
Desire him to walk up. I have your leave, I suppose, my lord?

[Exit **SERVANT**.

LORD NORLAND
Yes; but let me get out of the house without meeting him.

[Going to the opposite Door.

Can I go this way?

MR HARMONY
Why should you shun him?

LORD NORLAND
Because he used his wife ill.

MR HARMONY
He did. But I believe he is very sorry for it.—And as for you,—he said to me only a few hours ago—but no matter.

LORD NORLAND
What did he say? I insist upon knowing.

MR HARMONY
Why, then, he said, that if he had a sacred trust to repose in any one, you should be the man on earth, to whom he would confide it.

LORD NORLAND
Well, I am in no hurry; I can stay a few minutes.

[Enter **SIR ROBERT RAMBLE**.

SIR ROBERT
Oh! Harmony! I am in such a distracted state of mind—

[Seeing **LORD NORLAND**, he starts, and bows with the most humble Respect.

LORD NORLAND
Sir Robert, how do you do?

SIR ROBERT
My lord, I am pretty well.—I hope I have the happiness of seeing your lordship in perfect health.

LORD NORLAND
Very well, sir, I thank you.

SIR ROBERT
Indeed, my lord, I think I never saw you look better.

LORD NORLAND
Mr. Harmony, you and Sir Robert may have some business—I wish you a good morning.

MR HARMONY
No, my lord, I fancy Sir Robert has nothing particular.

SIR ROBERT
Nothing, nothing, I assure you, my lord.

LORD NORLAND
However, I have business myself in another place, and so you will excuse me.

[Going.

SIR ROBERT [Following him]
My lord—Lord Norland,—I trust you will excuse my inquiries.—I hope, my lord, all your family are well?

LORD NORLAND
All very well.

SIR ROBERT
Your little éléve,—Master Edward,—the young gentleman you have adopted—I hope he is well—

[Hesitating and Confused.

And—your ward,—Miss Wooburn—I hope, my lord, she is well?

LORD NORLAND
Yes, Sir Robert, Miss Wooburn is tolerably well.

SIR ROBERT
Only tolerably, my lord? I am sorry for that.

MR HARMONY
I hope, my lord, you will excuse my mentioning the subject; but I was telling Sir Robert just now of your intentions respecting a second marriage for that lady; but Sir Robert does not appear to approve of the design.

LORD NORLAND
What objection can he have?

SIR ROBERT
My lord, there are such a number of bad husbands;—there are such a number of dissipated, unthinking, unprincipled men!—And—I should be extremely sorry to see any lady with whom I have had the honour of being so closely allied, united to a man, who would undervalue her worth.

LORD NORLAND
Pray, Sir Robert, were you not then extremely sorry for her, while she was united to you?

SIR ROBERT
Very sorry for her, indeed, my lord. But, at that time, my mind was so much taken up with other cares, I own I did not feel the compassion which was her due; but, now that I am single, I shall have leisure to pay her more attention; and should I find her unhappy, it must, inevitably, make me so.

LORD NORLAND
Depend upon it, that, on the present occasion, I shall take infinite care in the choice of her husband.

SIR ROBERT
If your lordship would permit me to have an interview with Miss Wooburn, I think I should be able at least—

LORD NORLAND
You would not sure insult her by your presence?

SIR ROBERT
I think I should be able at least to point out an object worthy of her taste—I know that which she will like better than any one in the world.

LORD NORLAND
Her request has been, that I may point her out a husband the reverse of you.

SIR ROBERT

Then, upon my honour, my lord, she won't like him.

LORD NORLAND

Have not you liked women the reverse of her?

SIR ROBERT

Yes, my lord, perhaps I have, and perhaps I still do. I do not pretend to love her; I did not say, I did; nay, I positively protest I do not; but this indifference I acknowledge as one of my faults; and, notwithstanding all my faults, give me leave to acknowledge my gratitude that your lordship has nevertheless been pleased to declare—you think my virtues are numberless.

[**LORD NORLAND** shows Surprise.

MR HARMONY [Aside to **SIR ROBERT**]

Hush, hush!—Don't talk of your virtues now.

LORD NORLAND

Sir Robert, to all your incoherent language, this is my answer, this is my will: the lady, to whom I have had the honour to be guardian, shall never (while she calls me friend) see you more.

[**SIR ROBERT**, at this Sentence, stands silent for some Time, then, suddenly recollecting himself:

SIR ROBERT

Lord Norland, I am too well acquainted with the truth of your word, and the firmness of your temper, to press my suit one sentence farther.

LORD NORLAND

I commend your discernment.

SIR ROBERT

My lord, I feel myself a little embarrassed.—I am afraid I have made myself a little ridiculous upon this occasion—Will your lordship do me the favour to forget it?

LORD NORLAND

I will forget whatever you please.

MR HARMONY [Following him, whispers]

I am sorry to see you going away in despair.

SIR ROBERT

I never did despair in my life, sir; and while a woman is the object of my wishes, I never will.

[Exit.

LORD NORLAND

What did he say?

MR HARMONY
That he thought your conduct, that of a just and an upright man.

LORD NORLAND
To say the truth, he has gone away with better manners than I could have imagined, considering his jealousy is provoked.

MR HARMONY
Ah! I always knew he loved his wife, notwithstanding his behaviour to her; for, if you remember—he always spoke well of her behind her back.

LORD NORLAND
No, I do not remember it.

MR HARMONY
Yes, he did; and that is the only criterion of a man's love, or of his friendship.

[Enter a **SERVANT**.

SERVANT
A young gentleman is at the door, sir, inquiring for Lord Norland.

LORD NORLAND
Who can it be?

MR HARMONY
Your young gentleman from home, I dare say. Desire him to walk in. Bring him here.

[Exit **SERVANT**.

LORD NORLAND
What business can he have to follow me?

[Enter **EDWARD**.

EDWARD
Oh, my lord, I beg your pardon for coming hither, but I come to tell you something you will be glad to hear.

MR HARMONY
Good Heaven, how like his mother!

LORD NORLAND
Taking him by the Hand.] I begin to think he is—But he was not so when I first took him. No, no, if he had, he would not have been thus near me now;—but to turn him away because his countenance is a little changed, I think would not be right.

EDWARD [To **MR HARMONY**]
Pray, sir, did you know my mother?

MR HARMONY
I have seen her.

EDWARD
Did you ever see her, my lord?

LORD NORLAND
I thought, you had orders never to inquire about your parents?—Have you forgot those orders?

EDWARD
No, my lord;—but when this gentleman said, I was like my mother—it put me in mind of her.

MR HARMONY
You do not remember your mother, do you?

EDWARD
Sometimes I think I do. I think sometimes I remember her kissing me, when she and my father went on board of a ship; and so hard she pressed me—I think I feel it now.

MR HARMONY
Perhaps she was the only lady that ever saluted you?

EDWARD
No, sir, not by many.

LORD NORLAND
But, pray, young man, (to have done with this subject,) what brought you here? You seem to have forgot your errand?

EDWARD
And so I had, upon my word. Speaking of my mother, put it quite out of my mind.—But, my lord, I came to let you know, the robber, who stopped you last night, is taken.

LORD NORLAND
I am glad to hear it.

EDWARD
I knew you would, and therefore I begged to be the first to tell you.

MR HARMONY [To **LORD NORLAND**]
Should you know the person again?

LORD NORLAND
I cannot say, I should; his face seemed so much distorted.

MR HARMONY
Ay, wretched man! I suppose, with terror.

LORD NORLAND
No; it appeared a different passion from fear.

MR HARMONY
Perhaps, my lord, it was your fear, that made you think so.

LORD NORLAND
No, sir, I was not frightened.

EDWARD
Then, why did you give him your money?

LORD NORLAND
It was surprise, caused me to do that.

EDWARD
I wondered what it was! You said it was not fear, and I was sure it could not be love.

MR HARMONY
How has he been taken?

EDWARD
A person came to our steward, and informed against him—and, Oh! my lord, his poor wife told the officers, who took him, they had met with misfortunes, which she feared had caused a fever in her husband's head: and, indeed, they found him too ill to be removed; and so, she hoped, she said, that, as a man not in his perfect mind, you would be merciful to him.

LORD NORLAND
I will be just.

EDWARD
And that is being merciful, is it not, my lord?

LORD NORLAND
Not always.

EDWARD
I thought it had been.—It is not just to be unmerciful, is it?

LORD NORLAND
Certainly not.

EDWARD
Then it must be just, to have mercy.

LORD NORLAND

You draw a false conclusion.—Great as the virtue of mercy is, justice is greater still.—Justice holds its place among those cardinal virtues, which include all the lesser.—Come, Mr. Harmony, will you go home with me? And, before I attend to this business, let me persuade you to forget there is such a person in the world as Sir Robert Ramble, and suffer me to introduce you to Miss Wooburn, as the man who—

MR HARMONY

I beg to be excused—Besides the consideration of Sir Robert, I have another reason why I cannot go with you.—The melancholy tale, which this young gentleman has been telling, has cast a gloom on my spirits, which renders me unfit for the society of a lady.

LORD NORLAND

Now I should not be surprised, were you to go in search of this culprit and his family, and come to me to intreat me to forego the prosecution; but, before you ask me, I tell you it is in vain—I will not.

MR HARMONY

Lord Norland, I have lately been so unsuccessful in my petitions to you, I shall never presume to interpose between your rigour and a weak sufferer more.

LORD NORLAND

Plead the cause of the good, and I will listen; but you find none but the wicked for your compassion.

MR HARMONY [Speaking with unaffected Compassion]

The good, in all states, even in the very grasp of death, are objects of envy; it is the bad who are the only sufferers. There, where no internal consolation cheers, who can refuse a little external comfort?—And, let me tell you, my lord, that, amidst all your authority, your state, your grandeur, I often pity you.

LORD NORLAND

Good day, Mr. Harmony; and when you have apologized for what you have said, we may be friends again.

[Exit, leading off **EDWARD**.

MR HARMONY

Nay, hear my apology now. I cannot—no, it is not in my nature, to live in resentment, nor under the resentment of any creature in the world.

[Exit, following **LORD NORLAND**.

SCENE II

An Apartment at Lord Norland's

Enter **SIR ROBERT RAMBLE**, followed by a **SERVANT**.

SIR ROBERT

Do not say who it is—but say, a gentleman, who has some particular business with her.

SERVANT
Yes, sir.

[Going.

SIR ROBERT
Pray,—

[**SERVANT** returns.

You have but lately come into this service, I believe?

SERVANT
Only a few days, sir.

SIR ROBERT
You don't know me, then?

SERVANT
No, sir.

SIR ROBERT
I am very glad of it. So much the better.—Go to Miss Wooburn, with a stranger's compliments, who is waiting, and who begs to speak with her, upon an affair of importance.

SERVANT
Yes, sir.

[Exit.

SIR ROBERT
I wish I may die, if I don't feel very unaccountably! How different are our sensations towards our wives, and all other women! This is the very first time she has given me a palpitation since the honeymoon.

[Enter **MISS WOOBURN**, who starts on seeing Sir Robert;—he bows in great Confusion.

MISS WOOBURN [Aside]
Support me Heaven!

SIR ROBERT [Bows repeatedly, and does not speak till after many Efforts]
Was ever man in such confusion before his wife!

MISS WOOBURN
Sir Robert, having recovered, in some measure, from the surprise into which this intrusion first threw me, I have only to say,—that, whatever pretence may have induced you to offer me this insult, there is not any that can oblige me to bear with it.

[Going.

SIR ROBERT
Lady Ramb—
[Recalling himself]
Miss Woo—
[She turns]
Lady Ramble—
[Recalling himself again]
Miss Wooburn—Madam—You wrong me—There was a time when I insulted you, I confess; but it is impossible that time should ever return.

MISS WOOBURN
While I stay with you, I incur the danger.

[Going.

SIR ROBERT [Holding her]
Nay, listen to me, as a friend, whom you have so often heard as an enemy.—You offered me a favour by the hands of Mr. Harmony—

MISS WOOBURN
And is this the motive of your visit—this the return—

SIR ROBERT
No, madam, that obligation was not the motive which drew me hither—The real cause of this seeming intrusion is—you are going to be married once more, and I come to warn you of your danger.

MISS WOOBURN
That you did sufficiently in the marriage state.

SIR ROBERT
But now I come to offer you advice, that may be of the most material consequence, should you really be determined to yield yourself again into the power of a husband.

MISS WOOBURN
Which I most assuredly am.

SIR ROBERT
Happy, happy man! How much is he the object of my envy! None so well as I, know how to envy him, because none so well as I, know how to value you.

[She offers to go]

Nay, by Heaven, you shall not go, till you have heard all that I came to say!

MISS WOOBURN

Speak it then, instantly.

SIR ROBERT
No, it would take whole ages to speak; and should we live together, as long as we have lived together, still I should not find time to tell you—how much I love you.

[A loud Rapping at the Street Door.

MISS WOOBURN
That, I hope, is Lord Norland.

SIR ROBERT
And what has Lord Norland to do with souls free as ours? Let us go to Scotland again: and again bid defiance to his stern commands.

MISS WOOBURN
Be assured, that through him only, will I ever listen to a syllable you have to utter.

SIR ROBERT
One syllable only, and I am gone that instant.

MISS WOOBURN
Well, sir?

[He hesitates, trembles, seems to struggle with himself; then approaching her slowly, timidly, and, as if ashamed of his Humiliation, kneels to her—She turns away.

SIR ROBERT [Kneeling]
Maria, Maria, look at me!—Look at me in this humble state—Could you have suspected this, Maria?

MISS WOOBURN
No: nor can I conceive what this mockery means.

SIR ROBERT
It means, that, now you are no longer my wife, you are my goddess; and thus I offer you my supplication, that, (if you are resolved not to live single) amongst the numerous train who present their suit,—you will once more select me.

MISS WOOBURN
You!—You, who have treated me with cruelty; who made no secret of your love for others; but gloried, boasted of your gallantries.

SIR ROBERT
I did, I did—But here I swear, only trust me again—do but once more trust me, and I swear by all I hold most sacred, that I will, for the future, carefully conceal all my gallantries from your knowledge—though they were ten times more frequent than before.

[Enter **EDWARD**.

EDWARD
Oh, my dear Miss Wooburn—What! Sir Robert here too!

[Goes to **SIR ROBERT**, and shakes Hands.

How do you do, Sir Robert? Who would have thought of seeing you here? I am glad to see you, though, with all my heart; and so, I dare say, is Miss Wooburn, though she may not like to say so.

MISS WOOBURN
You are impertinent, sir.

EDWARD
What, for coming in? I will go away then.

SIR ROBERT
Do, do—there's a good boy—do.

EDWARD [Going, returns]
I cannot help laughing, though, to see you two together!—for you know you never were together when you lived in the same house.

SIR ROBERT
Leave the room instantly, sir, or I shall call Lord Norland.

EDWARD
Oh, don't take that trouble; I will call him myself.

[Runs to the Door.

My lord! my lord! pray come hither this moment—As I am alive, here is Sir Robert Ramble along with Lady Ramble!

[Enter **LORD NORLAND**.

[**SIR ROBERT** looks confounded—**LORD NORLAND** points to **EDWARD** to leave the Room.

[Exit **EDWARD**.

LORD NORLAND
Sir Robert, on what pretence do you come hither?

SIR ROBERT
On the same pretence as when I was, for the first time, admitted into your house; to solicit this lady's hand: and, after having had it once, no force shall compel me to take a refusal.

LORD NORLAND
I will try, however—Madam, quit the room instantly.

SIR ROBERT

My lord, she shall not quit it.

LORD NORLAND

I command her to go.

SIR ROBERT

And I command her to stay.

LORD NORLAND

Which of us will you obey?

MISS WOOBURN

My inclination, my lord, disposes me to obey you;—but I have so lately been accustomed to obey him; that custom inclines me to obey him still.

SIR ROBERT

There! there! there, my lord! Now I hope you will understand better for the future, and not attempt to interfere between a man and his wife?

LORD NORLAND To **MISS WOOBURN**]

Be explicit in your answer to this question—Will you consent to be his wife?

MISS WOOBURN

No, never.

SIR ROBERT

Zounds, my lord! now you are hurrying matters.—You should do it by gentle means;—let me ask her gently.—
[With a most soft Voice]
Maria, Maria, will you be my wife once again?

MISS WOOBURN

Never.

SIR ROBERT

So you said seven years ago, when I asked you, and yet you consented.

LORD NORLAND

And now, Sir Robert, you have had your answer; leave my house.

[Going up to him.

SIR ROBERT

Yes, sir; but not without my other half.

LORD NORLAND

Your other half?

SIR ROBERT
Yes; the wife of my bosom—the wife, whom I swore at the altar "to love and to cherish, and, forsaking all others, cleave only to her, as long as we both should live."

LORD NORLAND
You broke your oath, and made the contract void.

SIR ROBERT
But I am ready to take another oath, and another after that, and another after that—And, Oh! my dear Maria, be propitious to my vows, and give me hopes you will again be mine.

[He goes to her, and kneels in the most supplicating Attitude.

[Enter **EDWARD**, showing in **MR SOLUS** and **MR PLACID**. **EDWARD** points to **SIR ROBERT** (who has his Back to them) and goes off.

SIR ROBERT [Still on his Knees, and not perceiving their Entrance]
I cannot live without you.—Receive your penitent husband, thus humbly acknowledging his faults, and imploring you to accept him once again.

MR SOLUS [Going up to **SIR ROBERT**]
Now, is it wonderful that I should want a wife?

MR PLACID
And is it to be wondered at, if I should hesitate about parting with mine?

SIR ROBERT [Starts up in great Confusion]
Mr. Solus, Mr. Placid, I am highly displeased that my private actions should be thus inspected.

MR SOLUS
No one shall persuade me now, to live a day without a wife.

MR PLACID
And no one shall persuade me now, not to be content with my own.

MR SOLUS
I will procure a special licence, and marry the first woman I meet.

SIR ROBERT
Mr. Solus, you are, I believe, interested in a peculiar manner, about the marriage of this lady.

MR SOLUS
And, poor man, you are sick, and want somebody to bathe your temples, and to hover about you.

MISS WOOBURN
You come in most opportunely, my dear Mr. Solus, to be a witness—

SIR ROBERT
My dear Mr. Solus!

MR SOLUS
To be a witness, madam, that a man is miserable without a wife. I have been a fatal instance of that, for some time.

MISS WOOBURN
Come to me, then, and receive a lesson.

SIR ROBERT
No, madam, he shall not come to you; nor shall he receive a lesson. No one shall receive a lesson from you, but myself.

LORD NORLAND
Sir Robert, one would suppose, by this extraordinary behaviour, you were jealous.

SIR ROBERT
And so I am, my lord; I have cause to be so.

LORD NORLAND
No cause to be jealous of Mr. Solus—he is not Miss Wooburn's lover, I assure you.

SIR ROBERT
Then, my lord, I verily believe it is yourself. Yes, I can see it is; I can see it in her eyes, and by every feature in your face.

MISS WOOBURN
Oh! my good friend, Mr. Placid, only listen to him.

SIR ROBERT
And why, my good friend, Mr. Placid?—
[To **MR PLACID**]
By Heavens, sir, I believe that you only wished to get rid of your own wife, in order to marry mine.

MR PLACID
I do not wish to part with my own wife, Sir Robert, since what I have just seen.

SIR ROBERT [Going up to **MR SOLUS** and **LORD NORLAND**]
Then, pray, gentlemen, be so good as to tell me, which of you two is the happy man, that I may know how to conduct myself towards him?

MISS WOOBURN
Ha! ha! ha!

SIR ROBERT
Do you insult me, Maria?—Oh! have pity on my sufferings.

MR SOLUS
If you have a mind to kneel down again, we will go out of the room.

MR PLACID
Just as I was comforting myself with the prospect of a divorce, I find my instructor and director pleading on his knees to be remarried.

[Enter **MRS PLACID**, who steals upon **MR PLACID** unperceived.

MRS PLACID
What were you saying about a divorce?

SIR ROBERT
Now, down on your knees, and beg pardon.

MISS WOOBURN
My dear Mrs. Placid, if this visit is to me, I take it very kind.

MRS PLACID
Not absolutely to you, my dear. I saw Mr. Placid's carriage at the door, and so I stepped in to desire him to go home directly.

MR PLACID
Presently, my dear; I will go presently.

MRS PLACID
Presently won't do: I say, directly. There is a lady at my house in the greatest possible distress—
[Whispers him]
—Lady Eleanor—I never saw a creature in such distraction;
[Raising her Voice]
—therefore go home this moment; you shan't stay an instant longer.

MR SOLUS
Egad, I don't know whether I will marry or no.

MRS PLACID
Why don't you go, Mr. Placid, when I bid you?

MR SOLUS
No;—I think I won't marry.

MR PLACID
But, my dear, will not you go home with me?

MRS PLACID
Did not I tell you to go by yourself?

[**MR PLACID** bows, and goes off.

MR SOLUS
No;—I am sure I won't marry.

LORD NORLAND
And now, Mr. Solus and Sir Robert, these ladies may have some private conversation. Do me the favour to leave them alone.

MISS WOOBURN
My lord, with your leave, we will retire.

[Turns when she gets to the Door.

Sir Robert, I have remained in your company, and compelled myself to the painful task of hearing all you have had to say, merely for the satisfaction of exposing your love; and then enjoying the triumph, of bidding you farewell for ever.

[Exit with **MRS PLACID**.

MR SOLUS [Looking stedfastly at **SIR ROBERT**]
He turns pale at the thoughts of losing her. Yes, I think I'll marry.

LORD NORLAND
Come, Sir Robert, it is in vain to loiter; your doom is fixed.

SIR ROBERT [In a melancholy, musing Tone]
Shall I then never again know what it is to have a heart like hers, to repose my troubles on.

MR SOLUS
Yes, I am pretty sure I'll marry.

SIR ROBERT
—A friend in all my anxieties, a companion in all my pleasures, a physician in all my sicknesses—

MR SOLUS
Yes, I will marry.

LORD NORLAND
Come, come, Sir Robert, do not let you and I have any dispute.

[Leading him towards the Door.

SIR ROBERT
Senseless man, not to value those blessings—Not to know how to estimate them, till they were lost.

[**LORD NORLAND** leads him off.

MR SOLUS [Following]
Yes,—I am determined;—nothing shall prevent me—I will be married.

[Exit.

Enter **HAMMOND**, followed by **LADY ELEANOR**.

HAMMOND
My lord is busily engaged, madam; I do not suppose he would see any one, much less a stranger.

LADY ELEANOR
I am no stranger.

HAMMOND
Your name then, madam?

LADY ELEANOR
That I cannot send in. But tell him, sir, I am the afflicted wife of a man, who, for some weeks past, has given many fatal proofs of a disordered mind. In one of those fits of phrensy, he held an instrument of death, meant for his own destruction, to the breast of your lord (who by accident that moment passed,) and took from him, what he vainly hoped might preserve his own life, and relieve the wants of his family. But, his paroxysm over, he shrunk from what he had done, and gave the whole he had thus unwarrantably taken, into a servant's hands, to be returned to its lawful owner. The man, admitted to this confidence, betrayed his trust, and instead of giving up what was thus sacredly delivered to him, secreted it; and, to obtain the promised reward, came to this house, but to inform against the wretched offender; who now, only resting on your lord's clemency, can escape the direful fate he has incurred.

HAMMOND
Madam, the account you give, makes me interested in your behalf, and you may depend, I will repeat it all with the greatest exactness.

[Exit **HAMMOND**.

LADY ELEANOR [Looking round]
This is my father's house! It is only through two rooms and one short passage, and there he is sitting in his study. Oh! in that study, where I (even in the midst of all his business) have been so often welcome; where I have urged the suit of many an unhappy person, nor ever urged in vain. Now I am not permitted to speak for myself, nor have one friendly voice to do that office for me, which I have so often undertaken for others.

[Enter **HAMMOND**, **EDWARD** following.

HAMMOND
My lord says, that any petition concerning the person you come about, is of no use. His respect for the laws of his country demands an example such as he means to make.

LADY ELEANOR
Am I, am I to despair then?
[To **HAMMOND**]
Dear sir, would you go once more to him, and humbly represent—

HAMMOND
I should be happy to oblige you, but I dare not take any more messages to my lord; he has given me my answer.—If you will give me leave, madam, I'll see you to the door.

[Crosses to the other Side, and goes off.

LADY ELEANOR
Misery—Distraction!—Oh, Mr. Placid! Oh, Mr. Harmony! Are these the hopes you gave me, could I have the boldness to enter this house? But you would neither of you undertake to bring me here!—neither of you undertake to speak for me!

[She is following the **SERVANT**; **EDWARD** walks softly after her, till she gets near the Door; he then takes hold of her Gown, and gently pulls it; she turns and looks at him.

EDWARD
Shall I speak for you, madam?

LADY ELEANOR
Who are you, pray, young gentleman?—Is it you, whom Lord Norland has adopted for his son?

EDWARD
I believe he has, madam; but he has never told me so yet.

LADY ELEANOR
I am obliged to you for your offer; but my suit is of too much consequence for you to undertake.

EDWARD
I know what your suit is, madam, because I was with my lord when Hammond brought in your message; and I was so sorry for you, I came out on purpose to see you—and, without speaking to my lord, I could do you a great kindness—if I durst.

LADY ELEANOR
What kindness?

EDWARD
But I durst not—No, do not ask me.

LADY ELEANOR

I do not. But you have increased my anxiety, and in a mind so distracted as mine, it is cruel to excite one additional pain.

EDWARD

I am sure I would not add to your grief for the world.—But then, pray do not speak of what I am going to say.—I heard my lord's lawyer tell him just now, that, as he said he should not know the person again, who committed the offence about which you came, and as the man who informed against him is gone off, there could be no evidence that he did the action, but from a book, a particular pocketbook, of my lord's, which he forgot to deliver to his servant with the notes and money he returned, and which was found upon him at your house: and this Lord Norland will affirm to be his.—Now, if I did not think I was doing wrong, this is the very book—

[Takes a Pocketbook from his Pocket.

I took it from my lord's table;—but it would be doing wrong, or I am sure I wish you had it.

[Looking wishfully at her.

LADY ELEANOR

It will save my life, my husband's, and my children's.

EDWARD [Trembling]

But what is to become of me?

LADY ELEANOR

That Providence who never punishes the deed, unless the will be an accomplice, shall protect you, for saving one, who has only erred in a moment of distraction.

EDWARD

I never did any thing to offend my lord in my life;—and I am in such fear of him, I did not think I ever should.—Yet I cannot refuse you;—take it.—

[Gives her the Book.

But pity me, when my lord shall know of it.

LADY ELEANOR

Oh! should he discard you for what you have done, it will embitter every moment of my remaining life.

EDWARD

Do not frighten yourself about that.—I think he loves me too well to discard me quite.

LADY ELEANOR

Does he indeed?

EDWARD

I think he does!—for often, when we are alone, he presses me to his bosom so fondly, you would not suppose.—And, when my poor nurse died, she called me to her bedside, and told me (but pray keep it a secret)—she told me I was—his grandchild.

LADY ELEANOR
You are—you are his grandchild—I see,—I feel you are;—for I feel that I am your mother.

[Embraces him.

Oh! take this evidence back.

[Returning the Book.

—I cannot receive it from thee, my child;—no, let us all perish, rather than my boy, my only boy, should do an act to stain his conscience, or to lose his grandfather's love.

EDWARD
What do you mean?

LADY ELEANOR
The name of the person with whom you lived in your infancy, was Heyland?

EDWARD
It was.

LADY ELEANOR
I am your mother; Lord Norland's only child,

[**EDWARD** kneels.

—who, for one act of disobedience, have been driven to another part of the globe in poverty, and forced to leave you, my life, behind.

[She embraces and raises him.

Your father, in his struggles to support us all, has fallen a victim;—but Heaven, which has preserved my son, will save my husband, restore his senses, and once more—

EDWARD [Starting]
I hear my lord's step,—he is coming this way:—Begone, mother, or we are all undone.

LADY ELEANOR
No, let him come—for though his frown should kill me, yet must I thank him, for his care of thee.

[She advances towards the Door, to meet him.

[Enter **LORD NORLAND**.

[**LADY ELEANOR** falls on her Knees.

You love me,—'tis in vain to say you do not. You love my child; and with whatever hardship you have dealt, or still mean to deal by me, I will never cease to think you love me, nor ever cease my gratitude for your goodness.

LORD NORLAND
Where are my servants? Who let this woman in?

[She rises, and retreats from him, alarmed and confused.

EDWARD
Oh, my lord, pity her.—Do not let me see her hardly treated—Indeed I cannot bear it.

[Enter **HAMMOND**.

LORD NORLAND To **LADY ELEANOR**]
What was your errand here? If to see your child, take him away with you.

LADY ELEANOR
I came to see my father;—I have a house too full of such as he already.

LORD NORLAND
How did she gain admittance?

HAMMOND
With a petition, which I repeated to your lordship.

[Exit **HAMMOND**.

LORD NORLAND
Her husband, then, it was, who—
[To **LADY ELEANOR**]
But let him know, for this boy's sake, I will no longer pursue him.

LADY ELEANOR
For that boy's sake you will not pursue his father; but for whose sake are you so tender of that boy? 'Tis for mine, for my sake; and by that I conjure you—

[Offers to kneel.

LORD NORLAND
Your prayers are vain—
[To **EDWARD**]
Go, take leave of your mother for ever, and instantly follow me;—or shake hands with me for the last time, and instantly begone with her.

EDWARD [Stands between them in doubt for some little Time; looks alternately at each with Emotions of Affection; at last goes to his Grandfather, and takes hold of his Hand]
Farewell, my lord,—it almost breaks my heart to part from you;—but if I have my choice, I must go with my mother.

[Exit **LORD NORLAND** instantly.—**LADY ELEANOR** and her **SON** go off on the opposite Side.

SCENE II

Another Apartment at Lord Norland's

Enter **MISS WOOBURN** and **MRS PLACID**.

MRS PLACID
Well, my dear, farewell.—I have stayed a great while longer than I intended—I certainly forgot to tell Mr. Placid to come back after he had spoken with Lady Eleanor, or he would not have taken the liberty not to have come.

MISS WOOBURN
How often have I lamented the fate of Lord Norland's daughter! But, luckily, I have no personal acquaintance with her, or I should probably feel a great deal more on her account than I do at present.—She had quitted her father's house before I came to it.

[Enter **MR HARMONY**.

MR HARMONY
My whole life is passed in endeavouring to make people happy, and yet they won't let me do it.—I flattered myself, that after I had resigned all pretensions to you, Miss Wooburn, in order to accommodate Sir Robert—that, after I had told both my lord and him, in what high estimation they stood in each other's opinion, they would of course have been friends; or, at least not have come to any desperate quarrel:—instead of which, what have they done, but, within this hour, had a duel!—and poor Sir Robert—

MISS WOOBURN
For Heaven's sake, tell me of Sir Robert—

MR HARMONY
You were the only person he mentioned after he received his wound; and such encomiums as he uttered—

MISS WOOBURN
Good Heaven! If he is in danger, it will be vain to endeavour to conceal what I shall suffer.

[Retires a few Paces, to hide her Emotions.

MRS PLACID

Was my husband there?

MR HARMONY
He was one of the seconds.

MRS PLACID
Then he shall not stir out of his house this month, for it.

MR HARMONY
He is not likely; for he is hurt too.

MRS PLACID
A great deal hurt?

MR HARMONY
Don't alarm yourself.

MRS PLACID
I don't.

MR HARMONY
Nay, if you had heard what he said!

MRS PLACID
What did he say?

MR HARMONY
How tenderly he spoke of you to all his friends—

MRS PLACID
But what did he say?

MR HARMONY
He said, you had imperfections.

MRS PLACID
Then he told a falsehood.

MR HARMONY
But he acknowledged they were such as only evinced a superior understanding to the rest of your sex;—and that your heart—

MRS PLACID [Bursting into Tears]
I am sure I am very sorry that any misfortune has happened to him, poor, silly man! But I don't suppose—
[Drying up her Tears at once]
—he'll die.

MR HARMONY

If you will behave kindly to him, I should suppose not.

MRS PLACID

Mr. Harmony, if Mr. Placid is either dying or dead, I shall behave with very great tenderness; but if I find him alive, and likely to live, I will lead him such a life as he has not led a long time.

MR HARMONY

Then you mean to be kind?—But, my dear Miss Wooburn,—
[Going to her]
—why this seeming grief? Sir Robert is still living; and should he die of his wounds, you may at least console yourself, that it was not your cruelty which killed him.

MISS WOOBURN

Rather than have such a weight on my conscience, I would comply with the most extravagant of his desires, and suffer his cruelty to be the death of me.

MR HARMONY

If those are your sentiments, it is my advice that you pay him a visit in his affliction.

MISS WOOBURN

Oh no, Mr. Harmony, I would not for the universe. Mrs. Placid, do you think it would be proper?

MRS PLACID

No, I think it would not—Consider, my dear, you are no longer a wife, but a single woman, and would you run into the clutches of a man?

MR HARMONY

He has no clutches, madam; he is ill in bed, and totally helpless.—But, upon recollection, it would, perhaps, be needless to go; for he may be too ill to admit you.

MISS WOOBURN

If that is the case, all respect to my situation, my character, sinks before the strong desire of seeing him once more. Oh! were I married to another, I feel, that, in spite of all my private declarations, or public vows, I should fly from him, to pay my duty where it was first plighted.

MR HARMONY

My coach is at the door; shall I take you to his house? Come, Mrs. Placid, wave all ceremonious motives, on the present melancholy occasion, and go along with Miss Wooburn and me.

MISS WOOBURN

But, Mrs. Placid, perhaps poor Mr. Placid is in want of your attendance at home.

MR HARMONY

No, they were both carried in the same carriage to Sir Robert's.

MISS WOOBURN [As **MR HARMONY** leads her to the Door]

Oh! how I long to see my dear husband, that I may console him!

MRS PLACID
Oh! how I long to see my dear husband, that I may quarrel with him!

[Exeunt.

The Hall at Sir Robert Ramble's

The **PORTER** discovered asleep.

Enter a **FOOTMAN**.

FOOTMAN
Porter, porter, how can you sleep at this time of the day?—It is only eight o'clock.

PORTER
What did you want, Mr. William?

FOOTMAN
To tell you, my master must not be disturbed, and so you must not let in a single creature.

PORTER
Mr. William, this is no less than the third time I have received those orders within this half hour;—First from the butler, then from the valet, and now from the footman.—Do you all suppose I am stupid?

FOOTMAN
I was bid to tell you. I have only done what I was desired; and mind you do the same.

[Exit.

PORTER
I'll do my duty, I warrant you. I'll do my duty.

[A loud Rapping at the Door.

And there's a summons, to put my duty to the trial.

[Opens the Door.

[Enter **MR HARMONY**, **MISS WOOBURN**, and **MRS PLACID**.

MR HARMONY
These ladies come on a visit to Sir Robert. Desire one of the servants to conduct them to him instantly.

PORTER
Indeed, sir, that is impossible—My master is not—

MR HARMONY
We know he is at home, and therefore we can take no denial.

PORTER
I own he is at home, sir; but, indeed, he is not in a situation—

MISS WOOBURN
We know his situation.

PORTER
Then, madam, you must suppose he is not to be disturbed. I have strict orders not to let in a single soul.

MR HARMONY
This lady, you must be certain, is an exception.

PORTER
No lady can be an exception in my master's present state; for I believe, sir, but—perhaps, I should not speak of it—I believe my master is nearly gone.

MISS WOOBURN
Oh! support me, Heaven!

MRS PLACID
But has he his senses?

PORTER
Not very clearly, I believe.

MISS WOOBURN
Oh, Mr. Harmony, let me see him, before they are quite lost.

PORTER
It is as much as my place is worth, to let a creature farther than this hall; for my master is but in the next room.

MRS PLACID
That is a dining room. Is not he in bed?

MR HARMONY [Aside to the **LADIES**]
In cases of wounds, the patient is oftentimes propped up in his chair.

MISS WOOBURN
Does he talk at all?

PORTER

Yes, madam, I heard him just now very loud.

MISS WOOBURN [Listening]
I think I hear him rave.

MR HARMONY
No, that murmuring is the voice of other persons.

MRS PLACID
The physicians in consultation, I apprehend.—Has he taken any thing?

PORTER
A great deal, I believe, madam.

MRS PLACID
No amputation, I hope;

PORTER
What, madam?

MR HARMONY
He does not understand you.
[To **MISS WOOBURN**]
—Come, will you go back?

PORTER
Do, my lady, and call in the morning.

MISS WOOBURN
By that time he may be totally insensible, and die without knowing how much I am attached to him.

MRS PLACID
And my husband may die without knowing how angry I am with him!—Mr. Harmony, never mind this foolish man, but force your way into the next room.

PORTER
Indeed, sir, you must not. Pray, Mr. Harmony, pray, ladies, go away.

MISS WOOBURN
Yes, I must go from my husband's house for ever, never to see that, or him again!

[Faints on **MR HARMONY**.

MRS PLACID
She is fainting—open the windows—give her air.

PORTER
Pray go away:—There is plenty of air in the streets, ma'am.

MR HARMONY
Scoundrel! Your impertinence is insupportable. Open these doors; I insist on their being opened.

[He thrusts at a Door in the Centre of the Stage; it opens, and discovers **SIR ROBERT** and **MR PLACID** at a Table, surrounded by a **COMPANY OF GENTLEMEN**.

SIR ROBERT
A song—a song—another song—

[**MISS WOOBURN**, all astonishment, is supported by **MR HARMONY** and **MRS PLACID**.—The **PORTER** runs off.

Ah, what do I see!—Women!—Ladies!—Celestial beings we were talking of.—Can this be real?

[**SIR ROBERT** and **MR PLACID** come forward—**SIR ROBERT**, perceiving it is **MISS WOOBURN**, turns himself to the Company.

Gentlemen, gentlemen, married men and single men, hear me thus publicly renounce every woman on earth but this; and swear henceforward to be devoted to none but my own wife.

[Goes to her in Raptures.

MR PLACID [Looking at **MRS PLACID**, then turning to the **COMPANY**]
Gentlemen, gentlemen, married men and single men, hear me thus publicly declare, I will henceforth be master; and from this time forward, will be obeyed by my wife.

[**SIR ROBERT** waves his Hand, and the Door is closed on the **COMPANY OF GENTLEMEN**.

MRS PLACID
Mr. Placid—Mr. Placid, are you not afraid?

MR PLACID
No, madam, I have consulted my friends, I have drank two bottles of wine, and I never intend to be afraid again.

MISS WOOBURN [To **SIR ROBERT**]
Can it be, that I see you without a wound?

SIR ROBERT
No, my life, that you do not; For I have a wound through my heart, which none but you can cure. But, in despair of your aid, I have flown to wine, to give me a temporary relief by the loss of reflection.

MRS PLACID
Mr. Placid, you will be sober in the morning.

MR PLACID
Yes, my dear; and I will take care that you shall be dutiful in the morning.

MR HARMONY
For shame! how can you treat Mrs. Placid thus; you would not, if you knew what kind things she has been saying of you; and how anxious she was, when I told her you were wounded in a duel.

MRS PLACID
Was not I, Mr. Harmony?

[Bursting into Tears.

MR PLACID [Aside to **MR HARMONY** and **SIR ROBERT**]
I did not know she could cry;—I never saw it before, and it has made me sober in an instant.

MISS WOOBURN
Mr. Placid, I rely on you to conduct me immediately from this house.

SIR ROBERT
That I protest against: and will use even violent measures to prevent him.

[Enter a **SERVANT**.

SERVANT
Lord Norland.

[Enter **LORD NORLAND**.

MISS WOOBURN
He will protect me.

SIR ROBERT
Who shall protect you in my house but I? My lord, she is under my protection; and if you offer to take her from me, I'll exert the authority of a husband, and lock her up.

LORD NORLAND [To **MISS WOOBURN**]
Have you been deluded hither, and wish to leave the place with me? Tell me instantly, that I may know how to act.

MISS WOOBURN
My lord, I am ready to go with you, but—

MR HARMONY
But you find she is inclined to stay;—and do have some compassion upon two people, that are so fond of you.

[Enter **MR SOLUS**, dressed in a Suit of white Clothes.

MR SOLUS
I am married!—I am married!—Wish me joy! I am married!

SIR ROBERT
I cannot give you joy, for envy.

MR SOLUS
Nay, I do not know whether you will envy me much when you see my spouse—I cannot say she was exactly my choice. However, she is my wife now; and that is a name so endearing, that I think I love her better since the ceremony has been performed.

MRS PLACID
And pray when did it take place?

MR SOLUS
This moment. We are now returning from a friend's house, where we have been joined by a special licence; and I felt myself so happy, I could not pass Sir Robert's door without calling to tell him of my good fortune. And, as I see your lady here, Sir Robert, I guess you are just married too; and so I'll hand my wife out of the carriage, and introduce the two brides to each other.

[Exit **MR SOLUS**.

SIR ROBERT
You see, my lord, what construction Mr. Solus has put on Miss Wooburn's visit to me; and, by Heaven, if you take her away, it will be said, that she came and offered herself to me, and that I rejected her!

MISS WOOBURN
Such a report would kill me.

[Enter **MR SOLUS**, leading on **MISS SPINSTER**.

MR SOLUS
Mistress Solus.

[Introducing her.

MR HARMONY [Starting]
My relation! Dear madam, by what strange turn of fortune do I see you become a wife?

MRS SPINSTER
Mr. Harmony, it is a weakness, I acknowledge: but you can never want an excuse for me, when you call to mind the scarcity of provisions.

MR SOLUS
Mr. Harmony, I have loved her ever since you told me, she spoke so well of me behind my back.

[Enter **SERVANT**, and whispers **MR HARMONY**, who follows him off.

LORD NORLAND

I agree with you, Mr. Solus, that this is a most excellent proof of a person's disposition; and in consideration, Sir Robert, that throughout all our many disagreements, you have still preserved a respect for my character in my absence, I do at last say to that lady, she has my consent to trust you again.

SIR ROBERT
And she will trust me: I see it in her smiles. Oh! unexpected ecstacy!

[Enter **MR HARMONY**.

MR HARMONY [Holding a Letter in his Hand]
Amidst the bright prospects of joy, which this company are contemplating, I come to announce an event that ought to cloud the splendour of the horizon—A worthy, but an ill-fated, man, whom you are all acquainted with, has just breathed his last.

LORD NORLAND
Do you mean the husband of my daughter?

MR SOLUS
Do you mean my nephew?

MR PLACID
Is it my friend?

SIR ROBERT
And my old acquaintance?

MR HARMONY
Did Mr. Irwin possess all those titles you have given him, gentlemen? Was he your son?
[To **LORD NORLAND**]
Your nephew?
[To **MR SOLUS**]
Your friend?
[To **MR PALCID**]
And your old acquaintance?
[To **SIR ROBERT**]
How strange, he did not know it!

MR PLACID
He did know it.

MR HARMONY
Still more strange, that he should die for want, and not apply to any of you?

MR SOLUS
What! Die for want in London! Starve in the midst of plenty!

MR HARMONY

No; but he seized that plenty, where law, where honour, where every social and religious tie forbade the trespass; and, in punishment of the guilt, has become his own executioner.

LORD NORLAND
Then my daughter is wretched, and her boy involved in his father's infamy.

MR SOLUS
The fear of his ghost haunting me, will disturb the joys of my married life.

MR PLACID
Mrs. Placid, Mrs. Placid, my complying with your injunctions, in respect of Mr. Irwin, will make me miserable for ever.

MISS WOOBURN
I wish he had applied to me.

SIR ROBERT
And, as I refused him his request, I would give half my estate, that he had not applied to me.

MR HARMONY
And a man who always spoke so well of you all behind your backs!—I dare say that, in his dying moments, there was not one of you whom he did not praise for some virtue.

MR SOLUS
No, no—when he was dying, he would be more careful of what he said.

LORD NORLAND
Sir Robert, good day. Settle your marriage as you and your lady shall approve; you have my good wishes. But my spirits have received too great a shock, to be capable of any other impression at present.

MISS WOOBURN [Holding him]
Nay, stay, my lord.

MR SOLUS
And, Mrs. Solus, let me hand you into your carriage, to your company; but excuse my going home with you. My spirits have received too great a shock, to be capable of any other impression at present.

MR HARMONY [Stopping **MR SOLUS**]
Now, so loth am I to see any of you, only for a moment, in grief, while I have the power to relieve you, that I cannot help—Yes, my philanthropy will get the better of my justice.

[Goes to the Door, and leads in **LADY ELEANOR**, **MR IRWIN**, and **EDWARD**.

LORD NORLAND Runs to **MR IRWIN**, and embraces him]
My son!

[**MR IRWIN** falls on his Knees]

I take a share in all your offences—The worst of accomplices, while I impelled you to them.

MR IRWIN [On his Knees]
I come to offer my returning reason; to offer my vows, that, while that reason continues, so long will I be penitent for the phrensy which put your life in danger.

LADY ELEANOR [Moving timidly to her **FATHER**, leading **EDWARD** by the Hand]
I come to offer you this child, this affectionate child; who, in the midst of our caresses, droops his head, and pines for your forgiveness.

LORD NORLAND
Ah! there is a corner of my heart left to receive him.

[Embraces him.

EDWARD
Then, pray, my lord, suffer the corner to be large enough to hold my mother too.

LORD NORLAND
My heart is softened, and receives you all.

[Embraces **LADY ELEANOR**, who falls on her Knees; he then turns to **MR HARMONY**.

Mr. Harmony, I thank you, I most sincerely thank you, for this, the most joyful moment of my life. I not only experience release from misery, but return to happiness.

MR HARMONY [Goes hastily to **MR SOLUS**, and leads him to **MR IRWIN**; then turns to **MR and MRS PLACID**]
And now, that I see all you reconciled, I can say—there are not two enemies, in the whole circle of my acquaintance, that I have not, within these three days, made friends.

SIR ROBERT
Very true, Harmony: for we should never have known half how well we all love one another, if you had not told us.

MR HARMONY
And yet, my good friends, notwithstanding the merit you may attribute to me, I have one most tremendous fault; and it weighs so heavy on my conscience, I would confess what it is, but that you might hereafter call my veracity in question.

SIR ROBERT
My dear Harmony, without a fault, you would not be a proper companion for any of us.

LORD NORLAND
And whilst a man like you, may have (among so many virtues) some faults; let us hope there may be found in each of us (among all our faults) some virtues.

MR HARMONY

Yes, my lord,—and, notwithstanding our numerous faults, it is my sincere wish, that the world may speak well of us all—behind our backs.

Elizabeth Simpson was born on 15th October 1753 at Stanningfield, near Bury St Edmunds, Suffolk. She was the eighth of nine children to John Simpson, a farmer, and his wife, Mary, née Rushbrook. The family were Roman Catholics.

Her brother was educated at school, but Elizabeth, like her sisters, was educated at home. Elizabeth also suffered from a speech impediment, a stammer.

Elizabeth's father had died when she was only eight, leaving her mother to take care of a large family. These were difficult times.

Despite the fact that she suffered from a debilitating stammer she was determined, from a very young age, to become an actress. She had loved theatre from her very first childhood visit.

As a young woman Elizabeth was tall and slender. But this beauty brought with it the many attentions of men. It was double-edged.

Elizabeth had written to the manager of the Norwich Theatre to obtain acting work. He had replied that he would welcome a visit for her to audition. For her young naïve years this seemed like a golden opportunity. However, in 1770 her family forbade her attempt to take on an acting assignment there. They had no such qualms with her brother George, who entered the acting profession.

In April 1772, Elizabeth left, without permission, for London to pursue her chosen career. Although she was successful in obtaining parts her audiences found it difficult to admire her talents given her speech impediment. However, Elizabeth was diligent and hard-working on attempting to overcome this hurdle. She spent much time concentrating on pronunciation in order to eliminate the stammer. She was known to write out the parts she wanted to perform and practice the lines to point of such familiarity that her impediment was banished. Her acting, although at times stilted, especially in monologues, gained praise for her approach, and for her well-developed characters. For the audience she came across as a real person, not just an actor performing a piece. Elizabeth would keenly study the performances of others before she herself performed.

In these early months Elizabeth was young and alone, and reportedly also suffered from the attentions of sexual predators.

In June, merely two months after arriving she accepted an offer of marriage from Joseph Inchbald, a fellow Catholic and actor. They had met before on her previous trips to London, usually to see her brother, George, acting on stage. He had written her several letters proposing marriage which she had declined. But now it seemed the most expedient way to make progress in her career.

By all accounts it was still an odd choice. Joseph was a so-so actor, and at least twice her age as well as being the father of two illegitimate sons. The marriage was to produce no children and was not the happiest of unions.

On 4th September of that year, 1772, Elizabeth and Joseph appeared for the first time together on stage in 'King Lear'. The following month they toured Scotland with the West Digges's theatre company. This was to continue for the next four years.

In 1776 they decided on a change of career and a change of country. They moved to France. Joseph would now learn to paint, and Elizabeth would study French. It was a short-lived disaster. Within a month all their funds were gone and a return to England was necessitated.

They moved to Liverpool, Canterbury and Yorkshire and acted for both the Joseph Younger's company and Tate Wilkinson's company in search of permanency and a recovery from their ill-fortune.

Completely unexpectedly Joseph died in June 1779. Despite her loss Elizabeth continued to perform across the country from Dublin to London and places in between.

In 1780, she joined the Covent Garden Company and played Bellarion in 'Philaster'.

In all Elizabeth's acting career was only moderately successful and lasted some 17 years. However, she appeared in many classical roles as well as new plays such as Hannah Cowley's 'The Belle's Stratagem'. Around the theatre she was known for upholding high moral standards. She later described having to fend off sexual advances from, among others, stage manager James Dodd and theatre manager John Taylor.

It was now in the years after her husband's death that that Elizabeth decided on a new literary path. With no attachments, and acting taking up only some of her time, she decided to write plays.

Her first play to be performed was 'A Mogul Tale or, The Descent of the Balloon', in 1784, in which she also played the leading female role of Selina. The play was premiered at the Haymarket Theatre.

'Lovers' Vows', in 1798, was based on her translation of August von Kotzebues original work and garnered both praise and complements from Jane Austen and was featured as a focus of moral controversy in her novel Mansfield Park. Although Austen's book brought more fame to Elizabeth, 'Lovers' Vows' initially ran for only forty-two nights when originally performed in 1798.

One of the things that separated Elizabeth from other contemporary playwrights was her ability to translate plays from German and French into English and to use them as a foundation. These translations were popular with the public and her talents in bringing the characters to life was instrumental in achieving this.

Her success as a playwright enabled Elizabeth to support herself and not need a new husband to carry out this role. Between 1784 and 1805 she had 19 of her comedies, sentimental dramas, and farces (many of them translations from the French) performed at London theatres, although it is thought she actually wrote between 21 and 23 in total depending on which account you think is most accurate. She is usually credited as Mrs Inchbald.

As well she wrote two novels; 'A Simple Story' was published in 1791 and once referred to as "the most elegant English fiction of the eighteenth century". 'Nature and Art' was published in 1796. Both have been constantly reprinted.

Her four-volume autobiography was destroyed before her death upon the advice of her confessor, but she left a few of her diaries.

In her later years she found time to do a considerable amount of editorial and critical work. In 1805, she decided to try being a theatre critic. This literary excursion, after the praise for her acting and more so for her writing, seemed to be a low point in her achievements. The reception to her work amongst her peer critics was low, one commented upon her ignorance of Shakespeare.

Her career from actress, to playwright and novelist was achieved in difficult times for women to accomplish such things. Indeed, whilst the theatre and its boundaries were quite strict she managed, in her novels, to explore political radicalism. Her good looks together with her passionate and fiery nature attracted a string of admirers but she never re-married. Despite her love of independence, she still desired and sought social respectability.

Mrs Elizabeth Inchbald died on 1st August 1821 in Kensington, London.

She is buried in the churchyard of St Mary Abbots. On her gravestone is written, "Whose writings will be cherished while truth, simplicity, and feelings, command public admiration."

Mrs Inchbald – A Concise Bibliography

Plays
Mogul Tale; or, The Descent of the Balloon (1784)
Appearance is against Them (1785)
I'll Tell you What (1785)
The Widow's Vow (1786)
The Midnight Hour (1787)
Such Things Are (1787)
All on a Summer's Day (1787)
Animal Magnetism (c1788)
The Child of Nature (1788)
The Married Man (1789)
Next Door Neighbours (1791)
Everyone has his Fault (1793)
To Marry, or not to Marry (1793)
The Wedding Day (1794)
Wives as They Were and Maids as They Are (1797)
Lovers' Vows (1798)
The Wise Man of the East (1799)
The Massacre (1792 (not performed)
A Case of Conscience (published 1833)
The Ancient Law (not performed)

The Hue and Cry (unpublished)
Young Men and Old Women (Lovers No Conjurers) (adaptation of Le Méchant; unpublished)

Novels

A Simple Story (1791)
Nature and Art (1796)

www.ingramcontent.com/pod-product-compliance
Lightning Source LLC
Chambersburg PA
CBHW021937040426
42448CB00008B/1119